EXPERT UNRIVALLED

EXPERT UNRIVALLED

THE 5-STEP RECIPE FOR COACHES AND EXPERTS TO BECOME THE MOST DESIRED OPTION IN THE MARKET

Jen Hall

First published by Jen Hall in 2018

CONTENTS

With thanks to... viii
Important before you begin... xi
Introduction.. xiii

INGREDIENT 1: GRIT

1: The Pearl Transformation 6
2: Believe in You...12
3: Positive Action 16
4: How much? 26

INGREDIENT 2: PURPOSE

5: Turning Purpose into Profit 31
6: Discovering Your Purpose..35
7: Your Core Message 40
8: Your Mission 45

INGREDIENT 3: THE GLASS

9: Choosing the Right Glass 51
10: Niche Fear 55
11: How to Pick the Right Niche 59
12: 4 Step Method to Define Your Micro-Niche 61

INGREDIENT 4: MAGIC

13: The Truth About Magic..77
14: Keeping the Magic Alive..79
15: How to be Wanted 82

INGREDIENT 5: INTEGRITY

16: Authenticity - The Art of Integrity...................................91

17: How To Get Noticed 93
18: The Art of Being You 97
19: Know, Like, Trust 104
Next Steps 107
About the Author 108
Recommended Reading 110

Jen Hall - Business Coach, Author and Multi-Award Winning Speaker

With thanks to...

My daughter Ellie who brings meaning to my life beyond any words, and always brings me such immense happiness.

Special thanks to Andy Moore, my amazing partner who has supported beyond the call of duty and allowed me to take the risks, do the work and be the wild me! And loved me even when I'm being an unreasonable so and so.

I'd also like to share thanks to my family and friends who have supported me by not only proof reading this book, but more than that, they have supported me with love on my entrepreneurial journey and with great understanding on the time it takes to dedicate to my endeavours.

A huge thank you to Jessica Lorimer my coach and dearest friend, this book probably wouldn't have happened without her support. A fair share of this book has been inspired by her incredible work. She's changed my life on a serious scale and I want to share and mark my gratitude in this book.

To Helen Packham for helping me harness my story to make this book way more enjoyable to read than it would have been without her talented guidance.

To Keirsten Clark , book planning genius, who helped me map this baby out and kept me steady.

To my clients who make what I do possible! Without you, my life wouldn't be as soul fulfilled as it is. Many of you have become friends and have made bonds too strong to break. You leave more of an impact on me than you'll ever know.

To everyone who has supported me along the way, friends,

clients and followers! Without you, I couldn't be me. I am grateful for every message, email open, like, comment, share and supportive shoulder to cry on when things get tough. Because they do. You make my amazing journey possible and I'll continue to make it my mission make your journey just as amazing.

Thank you for being YOU!

I'm truly excited for you to be reading my first ever book! In fact, you are one of the first people to receive a copy of the very first print run! It's important to note that I wrote this entirely by my own fair hands and as mentioned you are part of a select few first readers. This also means that you may experience, on occasion, poor use of grammar, and that despite proof reading efforts, there may well be a few typos. I am not a seasoned author, so I hope you can forgive the odd error and see past the mistakes to appreciate the value, heart and soul that has gone into creating this book.

All I ask is that if you do spot any errors or would like to contribute feedback, if you wouldn't mind popping an email to jen@jen-hall.com to let me know I'd be truly grateful!

DO know this...

If you implement what I'm about to show you in this book, it *will* change your life and your business forever! This is a big promise to make, but one that I am 100% confident in making.

Happy reading!

IMPORTANT BEFORE YOU BEGIN...

Before you begin I want you to do something. Taking action and implementing what you discover inside this book will be key to your success in becoming a highly sought-after unrivalled expert.

As such, I have created an incredible interactive playbook where you can keep a record and note down ideas and progress as you go along. I am just as excited to share this FREE resource with you as I am you reading this book. All you have to do to access and download your FREE Expert Unrivalled Playbook, is visit www.jen-hall.com/expertunrivalledplaybook

Within the playbook you will find interactive questions that will help to pull the information and your own clarity together to start putting it into practice.

After each chapter I suggest you use your playbook to keep track of your progress and discoveries so you can build upon the clarity that comes to mind and fine-tune your unique excellence.

And just whilst you're here, please do read the introduction;

I myself have a tendency to skip introductions because I want to get to the juicy stuff. But I'm not a natural waffler and I've got straight to the point to deliver the good stuff so you won't waste time reading something that doesn't add value. The introduction is an important part of this journey and your education to becoming an unrivalled expert, so start from the beginning and work your way through and you'll find that you take away incredible insights that will change your life and business forever.

INTRODUCTION

Same Does Not Sell

It's June 2016 and I've just finished plastering Facebook with what feels like a million posts. I've posted in every Facebook group going, joined 10 more and watched as each post joined the other million posts just like it.

Still, that's the way it's done, right? It's clear that's the way it's done because everyone is doing it, so it must work. 'Perseverance is what's needed,' I thought to myself.

My goal was clear in my sights, I was ready to become the go-to expert, but I knew it would take time and I was willing to do what ever it took. Great attitude, right? That's grit right there. But it's one thing to follow a strategy and another to follow the crowd.

The biggest lesson I learned in 2016 was that 'same' does not sell.

I also learned that not every strategy is a 'proven to work strategy.' The strategy at that time, of posting inspirational quotes, 'look at me and my life' videos and value posts that shouted at people instead of engaging with them, was impersonal, samey, slimy and arrogant as hell. I mean who wants to listen to someone spout shite on Facebook every few minutes? Visibility isn't going to work if you're being visible with a ton of crap. You run the risk of becoming known for being the one to avoid or worse, you won't be noticed at all. Herding in the same direction as the other coaches coming off the conveyor belt, just isn't going to cut it. I realised that to stand out of the intense saturation online, I had to be different, I had to be unique and catch the attention of my ideal clients for the right reasons.

It also became apparent that millions of followers didn't always mean you were able to make money (monetise) from them. There are plenty of 'stars' out there with large followings that don't manage to monetise their audience. It was clear, I was playing in the wrong field, with the wrong team and the wrong fans.

'Focusing in' to go big, would be my new strategy. Quality over quantity. Specificity instead of everything. Somewhere instead of everywhere. Small and powerful instead of large and lost. Unique over generic. The exact strategy I used to package myself up as the unique, go-to expert I am today, is here inside this book.

I no longer look over my shoulder in concern for what others are doing, only to keep my eyes out for points of difference to reaffirm my unique stand point and for collaboration opportunities.

Visibility is still an important part of my success, in fact it's how I'm scaling my success, but showing up as the unique, highly valuable expert is what allows you to make the biggest impact and an epic income. Visibility is only the megaphone used to scale your profile and your message. A vague, fluffy, boring, samey profile and message will not get any better with more eyes on you. It's time to sharpen up, focus in and uncover your unique excellence to become an unrivalled expert.

Money, In The Case of the Entrepreneur, DOES Buy Happiness

Rewinding back in my journey before I started coaching - I'm 19 and I'm ready to be my own boss, and the first attempt at creating a successful business begins. I have always been interested in being my own boss having grown up watching my uncles and dad run their own businesses. I wanted to create a successful enterprise that my parents would be proud of and so that I could live unchained to society and be free to move around in my own life freely.

I've been reading business books since the age of 18 and as soon as I had enough information to run with, I was off. The first piece of advice any 'start your own business' book would give, is that before you start, you need to ensure that you follow your passion. It would dictate that without passion for what you do, your business would never survive. That exact advice resonated so much truth within me. I have always been a believer in everyone being on this earth for a reason, that we should all be living our life's purpose and if we could build a business around that we would be aligned enough to see success happen; as long as we persevered of course.

I started my career as an Entrepreneur at the age of 19 and have since ran six different businesses on my journey to become a successful business owner. Some of these businesses lasted longer than others with many more ideas that never made it out the gate.

Before each business attempt began, I would think about how I could turn my current life's passion into a business. Party host turned Event Planner, aromatherapy lover turned Complementary Therapist, business networker turned Network Event Leader, life's purpose believer turned Life Coach.

You will probably be wondering why so many businesses?

The reason - I simply couldn't find a sustainable interest. I couldn't create the balance between enjoying the journey and creating the financial success I wanted.

What these start up books *don't* tell you, is that if you struggled to make money from your passion, your once beloved past time would become a frustrating thorn in your side and a burden heavier that all the weights in the world.

I read books that yelled about action taking, how to create goals and hit them, why businesses fail and succeed, the best sales strategies, marketing your business, how to be more mindful about your work, how to make financial projections, how to write a business plan to receive investment and even 'The Dummies Guides to ....' But none of them told me what I'm about to reveal inside this book.

Failure is only possible when you give up, and I'll admit, I gave up on many occasions because the journey to success was hard work. Not just any old hard work, the kind of hard work that likens trying to fill a well using a bucket without a bottom. The kind of hard work and struggle that would see you in tears. I used to beat myself up over failure, because I knew that I was the one in control of it. I knew that giving up was the true failure. And I gave up. And that was my fault. I held onto these moments of giving up, beat myself up and they laid heavy in my heart for the longest time. And all because I didn't know the truth.

The gurus will tell you that hard work is how you build a business and I'd have to agree. But the truth of the matter is, hard work shouldn't be fruitless. Most people aren't really afraid of hard work; they're scared of the failure. They're pissed off with banging their head on a brick wall with nothing to show for it and they're scared of struggling to keep their head above water to support themselves and their family. True entrepreneurs are not scared of hard work, in fact most hungry and driven entrepreneurs will even enjoy hard work and often struggle to slow down and stop. Hard work is enjoyable when you're seeing the fruits of your labour. Running a business becomes a burden when it's taking more than you can give without the monetary return you want.

Every time something doesn't pull off as I want it to, it's a lesson. The reason I gave up was because I didn't know *how* to counteract it. I didn't *know* there was another way. Now, if something doesn't work, I change the plan not the goal. I've written this book not so you can put on a carbon copy cloak, I've written this in such a way that you can use this approach *your* way. Putting your stamp on how you operate and show up is vital to standing out. I want to tell you with every fibre of my being, that if you truly want to become a financially successful go-to expert, it is totally possible, no giving up is required. There is *always* a way.

The Reasons for My Struggle

1. I was a selfish ass-hole! I wanted to create a business that would serve *me*. I wanted control over how I spent my time, I wanted financial freedom, to do what I loved, to be my own boss, to quit my horrible job, to have something that would work around my lifestyle and children... I want, I want I want. 'I want' is no basis for a successful business. This only proves as a motivation for starting a business. The success of that business lies in the need you fulfil for others.

2. I wanted to maximise profits and help everyone by serving as many different people as I could. Ok, so the last half isn't so selfish, but I'd be lying if I said that helping more people didn't bring up the $$$ signs in my eyes. I am a born entrepreneur after all. But the problem is, serving everyone isn't possible and it won't bring in the money

either. This might sound very strange and may not add up for you at this exact moment, but this exact point is the reason my business is so successful today. More on this later.

3. I hid behind my business name, qualifications and techniques. In my head, a business name would make my business 'look bigger' than it was, it would look more professional and people would trust my business more.

This isn't wrong, but being totally transparent, I used it to hide behind. Essentially, I was saying to myself that I wasn't good enough or valuable enough to step out as me. Too scared to step out as an expert because who on earth would trust me? News flash – *you* are the business and people buy from people. These days I'm not afraid to be known as an expert and for *my* name, Jen Hall and being me.

4. I tried to give away my time for money. This left me overworked and hating the once loved hobbies and passions. Not only was I trading time for money, but I was also undercharging for my most valuable asset - time. There is always going to be a glass ceiling if you're doing everything yourself and you trade your time for money. There are only ever 24 hours in a day and if you're maxing out on delivery, you'll be leaving no time for marketing which creates a feast and famine pattern in your business. It's also impossible to scale on this model. One of my biggest business lessons and biggest business wins was to stop charging time for money and move to a 'charge for the results' model.

5. But the biggest reason for my failure was that people didn't want me. They didn't want me or what I had to offer. This still brings a lump to my throat stating this. It gets severely personal when you have to admit that in

reality the reason for your lack of income, is rejection of what you're trying to offer. Being a business owner, it can be hard to separate yourself from the business - because essentially the business is you and you are responsible for its' success.

It's well documented that the biggest reason for business failure is that the market fails to see a need for what you have to offer. What we're not told, is how to create something that *is* wanted by the market. We've been left to flounder and struggle for too long without the help and without the cold hard truth that we need to here. I'm here to deliver you the truth about being wanted in the market, and not just wanted but being the BEST option out there.

The truth is, with positioning, you *can* be wanted. And the best part is, I'm going to show you HOW!

Why this book?

If you haven't already resonated from my story so far, I'm going to tell you plain as day who this book is for.

This book is written for anyone who knows in their heart they are here to add an incredible amount of value to peoples' lives.

I'm talking to the intelligent women and men who have incredible expertise that are going unnoticed and unused.

It's written for those who once questioned their place in this world and doubted their worth but who are now ready to stand in their power and own their value.

This book is for you, so you can finally piece together the puzzle and collect the ingredients to become the go-to expert in your field.

There are no new ideas, every market is officially saturated, but the good news is, there is only one 'YOU' and when we can communicate what makes us so uniquely excellent, the saturation and competition no longer matter. You're able to position yourself as an unrivalled expert!

This book is designed to help you position yourself as the best option in the marketplace, so you can build a tribe of perfect prospects to not only monetize, but to impact each and every one of those lives!

This book is not designed to make you famous. There is a big difference between being famous and being known. You may be surprised to hear that in order to make impact and money, starting with a small exclusive group of people is essential to your long-term success. I am well known in my circles as THE Go-To Expert for clarity, micro-niche and positioning yourself as the best option in the marketplace. However, I am certainly not famous.

You don't need to be known by everyone - just the people that matter. To put it into perspective, Tony Robbins makes around $500 million a year and it's growing, but not *everyone* knows

him, because not everyone cares about what he's doing. It's highly unlikely that you'll ever reach a point where every person on the planet knows of your existence. Be comforted knowing that there are plenty of 7 figure coaches out there that you've never heard of but are well known in the circles, networks and communities that matter. Being famous does not make you money. Being well known for being worth knowing in the right circles is what will make more impact to the people you're meant to help and will ultimately make you more money.

The Starting Place

The words that seeded the direction of my current business were spoken at a networking event that I was attending about 4 years ago. The words spoken were as follows – 'everyone is no one in business'.

These few words brought everything into perspective and it all became clear for me. One of the biggest reasons for my business struggle and my previous business failures were glaringly obvious.

At the time of this networking event, the business I was running was a holistic practice offering varying services from massage, reflexology, aromatherapy to life coaching. The business was doing well from the current pool of clients but was struggling for new business. Of course, those that liked a firm targeted massage with medicinal oils that focused on relieving sleep problems, came back again and again because naturally they were getting what they wanted. The problem was, my marketing mentioned NOTHING about this specialism. I was trying to serve everyone instead of 'someone', just in case I cut out potential business. The fear of niching had a hold of me good and proper, and the result of this meant that the only clients I could attract were clients who came to me because of price, convenience and testimonials. Competing on price is a game you will ALWAYS lose, and the best experts are never convenient or cheap. The best experts are those that you'll happily wait for and rearrange your calendar to fit them in, and save or find the money to pay them. And of course, testimonials are great, but testimonials are the proof that tips the prospect to buy, not the leading sales hook that grabs their attention.

In terms of life coaching... jeeze, I had to bend people's arms to let me help them. Massage at least had a certain appeal and people already have the desire to feel more relaxed, but life coaching, what the fuck was that? Communicating the value of life coaching without a focus on the specific outcome and the specific problem I solved was like trying to convince people to take a pill and see what happens. Too weird, too scary and no flipping idea what it was going to do for them. Most of the people that I attracted were those who were curious about what life coaching could do, but curiosity doesn't sell. Without a destination for them to reach, they didn't know where the coaching was taking them, and NEITHER did I. I wasn't adding the value I knew I could and I wasn't delivering anything 'solid' to them to show for it, so out of integrity I pulled the plug on those services.

Sitting there at the networking event, this truth washed over me, and something else became clear. I didn't WANT anymore massage clients... I was tired and burnt out and felt like no money was worth the exhausting effort I was putting in. I knew that there was always going to be a ceiling on how many people I could cope with and physically fit into the schedule, which would always mean a ceiling on finances. Coaching was something that I was so passionate about and I knew I could scale it if I could just crack my niche.

So, I started reading, researching, attending business events, learning from business coaches, taking business courses in pursuit of niche marketing. This knowledge was powerful and one door after another of possibility and business mastery opened. But I didn't stop there, I became obsessed with learning about business success strategies, in particular - niching. I was learning that niching was a critical strategy for success, that no matter what business you are in, niching would make your marketing irresistible. This intensive and continual learning has never stopped, it truly is an obsession for me. I fell in love with the art of mastering successful service-based business and watched in awe of those who used the same successful strategies and techniques to build big impact and life changing businesses.

I applied my learning as soon as I could, and I started to market my coaching to people who wanted to discover their life's purpose for a career change. This immediately felt better, my energy changed, and I suddenly became excited about the possibility for my clients. My prospects became excited about the possibility of ditching their hum drum job to live their purpose, and from this aligned niche I finally started to attract clients instead of chasing them down.

The more I learned, the more I applied, and the more success I was seeing both in the ease of attraction and the interest in what I was offering. But I could sense something was shifting, I no longer wanted to work with people who wanted a job or even a small business, I wanted to work with those who dared to dream big, where small played no part in their plans. I had to get really honest with myself; I wanted to work with those who shared the same values I did- courage, integrity and self-worth. I wanted to work with those who wanted to build a money making business that changed lives. This was no longer just about living your purpose and passion, it became my mission to help those that wanted it all, the purpose, the passion, the life changing impact AND the money. And so, with the amazing help of the confidence and credibility queen Sanae Floyd, I stepped into my purpose, owned my knowledge and expertise, and finally embraced the label of Business Coach.

Something to note before we begin...

'People who pay, pay attention.' – Russell Brunson

I'm not ashamed to say that I love making money. From the days I used to struggle to pull £20 out of someone's hand to pay for my coaching, I know too well that if you're not selling, you're not serving. People need to WANT to pay for your services in order to truly invest themselves into the process. I can honestly say that the bigger the stretch (mindset speaking) to invest a large sum of money, the bigger the results and transformation for the person. When someone makes a big investment into themselves, I get seriously excited because I know good things are about to happen. If I'm not generating money in my business, I know I'm not making the impact I want to make. Freebie hunters will consume and sit, paying clients will consume and act. True impact only happens when someone takes action on the impact *you* make on them.

In this book we will be covering a lot on your micro-niche and ideal client, but one thing I want to seed into your brain right now, is that an ideal client is someone who can afford to pay you. If they can't they're not ideal and you're running a charity, not a business.

If I'm not making money in my business I can't continue to help people in the way that I do. If I'm not making money in my business I can't give up my time to spend with those who can't afford my services.

If you're here to earn serious money from your passion to serve others, then this is the book for you. I'm not saying we shouldn't be helping those that need us the most, we absolutely should, but you must be able to sustain yourself in your business in order to help those who can't pay. There is also a big difference between those that can't pay and won't pay. You cannot judge people for their financial situation. How much money they have or haven't got is really none of your business. What I mean by this is that many people including myself have found the money when they supposedly hadn't 'got it'. People WILL pay for what they value and for what they believe is possible. It's our job to communicate the value and the transformation possible for them, if you can't do this effectively, it doesn't matter how talented you are at what you do, you'll struggle to gain clients and ultimately struggle to make impact and become known for being worth knowing.

You need to inspire your clients to believe in the possibility of the transformation available and that you have what they need to get to their success island.

The Cocktail

In the digital age it has become harder and harder to be unique. People doing business with you just because you're local is something that is dying out. Once upon a time competition only existed 'down the road' and you only had to outshine but a few, but these days you're at the mercy of the entire connected world. The internet has brought us all closer together, but this has changed the entire landscape of how we used to do business and has made it more challenging for us to be the unique offering and find a niche that is totally our own.

Whilst niching is still vitally important to your success, it's become even more important to find your micro-niche. It's also important to realise that there is in fact more to being unique than *just* your micro-niche.

Being 'local' means absolutely nothing when the 'EXPERT' on the other side of the world is at our fingertips. The internet has dramatically changed how we do business and we must recognise that being local is no longer a benefit.

In fact, being local in some cases can actually put you at a disadvantage. Your lack of accessibility i.e. unable to provide services other than face to face, and lack of business ingenuity can blind the perception of your credibility in people's minds. People want to see you are a business that moves with the times. An expert that is at the forefront of their business is someone who cares about their success and cares about their clients.

Once you become an unrivalled expert and open up your reach to a wider focused community using the internet, being able to see you in person will prove to be a novelty and something that's highly valuable. You'll see that instead of being a convenience to visit, you'll be a MUST SEE regardless of the inconvenience of geography.

'The cocktail' is a concept I created to explain your USP (unique selling proposition). A cocktail is made up of several different elements to create a unique blend and this book serves as a recipe to your uniqueness and to your desirability factor to become a highly sought-after expert in your field and I can't wait for you to get stuck in!

The Cocktail Concept

"You can copy all you want, but you'll always be one step behind the originator."

There are some aspects to copying which I agree with. Copying proven strategies for instance is a smart move, along with copying a format that works. However, becoming a carbon copy of someone else means that not only will you always be one step behind, you'll be in direct competition and you'll always be sloppy seconds.

Besides, if you're copying someone, I'd assume it was because they were good right? So why would the consumer pick you over someone who is already rocking that corner?

When you do your own thing, you'll be something new and amazing to that market. There WILL be others out there doing a similar thing to you, they'll be on a similar mission, in a similar micro-niche, with similar values, but I'll tell you this as well, they won't be the same.

We are all different unique cocktails and instead of trying to replicate what's already been done, which is more exhausting than it looks, and becoming a weak, diluted version -concentrate on being YOU!

You are uniquely excellent in all your glory and in all your flaws. Own it all, don't be boring, be the anomaly and kick ass because you know what?

The world ain't seen nothin' yet!

What to expect...

This book is laid out in sections of each element/ingredient of your 'cocktail,' some of you will be stronger in some areas than others but know this; many people are strong in one area but very few master every single one. Your mastery in each area will be what sets you apart from everyone else, it will create your USP and will skyrocket you from ordinary to extraordinary.

I'd recommend reading the book once in order, and then feel free to read the book in which ever order you please but it's imperative that you master each area to become a unique, unrivalled, in-demand expert. Clarity can appear at any given moment, so keep reading and implementing and those light bulb moments are sure to appear.

Within this book there is something, that if harnessed, will accelerate your success to a limitless level, once you've read the book, I suggest you read it once more to really let the information sink in, and then read it once more taking your time to action each section.

What are you going to take away?

In this book I am going to show you the 'what' and the 'how' to become an unrivaled highly sought-after expert in your field.

You're going to learn the key steps you need to make competition obsolete and banish comparisons once and for all!

Imagine truly feeling like the expert and positioning yourself as the best option out there. That's one powerful position to be in.

This is not about bashing competition to get to the top. Surprisingly, neither is it about being 'better' than everyone else. This is about packaging you up as an irrefutable offering to the marketplace. Not everyone will buy from you, because not everyone is meant to be your client. We are going to identify who your ideal client is and make you totally irresistible for their eyes only! There shouldn't be too many more weird innuendos I promise.

'There is more than enough for everyone.'

You might want to chant this like a mantra if you find yourself living in the scarcity mindset that we're all fighting over clients.

By mastering the art of becoming the unrivalled expert you'll be in your lane, doing your thing and attracting your ideal clients with ease. Don't worry about anyone else!

INGREDIENT 1: GRIT

1

The Pearl Transformation

Today I can declare that I own something highly valuable and 'one of a kind'. There isn't another one like it, it's completely unique and even better, it's impossible to steal it, recreate it and its value is priceless. No, I'm not talking about bitcoin!

What's even weirder is that it started as a tiny piece of grit that found its way into an oyster. The oyster saw this grit as an irritant and so it secreted a liquid substance that coated the grit in an attempt to avoid irritation. The end result - a highly valuable, one of a kind pearl.

This pearl is the key to my success and has enabled me to help countless people achieve their own success.

I'd like to tell you a true story about someone I knew. For over 10 years she played it safe. For over 10 years she stood on the side lines admiring all those who were brave enough to own their expertise. For over 10 years she chose to hide from her true desire to stand up and be seen as someone who changed lives and made an epic difference in the world. The desire to make her dent and become (not famous) but well known for being worth knowing was burning strong. But there was just one tiny, huge problem... Every time she plucked up some courage to answer her calling, it was snuffed out by the questions of...

'Who would trust me to help them, let alone pay me to help them?

What do I have to offer?'

The questions became deafening statements – 'I don't have the qualifications to do this!

I don't know what I'm doing!

I don't have any credibility to do this!

I don't have anything worth paying for!

I'm not like all those others who have something that people truly care about.

Besides I could never be as great as them.'

She felt utterly worthless, but none the less that passion to do more, be more and make a difference never went away, not even for a second.

I'm going to stick my neck out and say that you will most likely relate to these feelings either now or at some point in your journey. I'm pleased to tell you that this story doesn't end here, this woman is now well known for being worth knowing, she changes the lives of others and earns her incredible value, and her story has only just begun.

I'd like to introduce this woman to you now. If you hadn't already guessed, which I'm sure you have, this woman is in fact me.

No one is immune to feeling this way, we all have the ability and weakness to, on some level, beat the crap out of ourselves with negative self-talk. Like everyone, I grew up in an environment that conditioned the way I viewed the world and the reality in which I lived. I grew up in my own little world where financial success was hard to come by, I was taught that it only came to the those who were willing to compromise happiness and health or to those who were lucky enough to know the right people. I grew up with the belief that failure was painful and something to avoid at all costs. This belief taught me never to take emotional risks and resulted in the fear of doing anything that might not work out. I was unconsciously conditioned by those around me to play it safe, follow the majority and take the easy route to save face. This was obviously a huge a problem and the weight of this fear and the lack of integrity to own my worth kept me held down for the longest time. It resulted in depression, frustration, a career that was a roller-coaster of highs and lows and a series of businesses that failed one after the other.

Every failure hung around my neck like unbearable weights. The worst part was, I wore these weights like medallions. Every morning I'd put them on. I liked wearing them because it was the heavy reminder of the pain of what happens when you put yourself out there. These weights kept me safe; small but safe.

But how does someone go from this self-deprecation to discovering and owning their awesomeness?

I wish I could say it was an easy journey for me, it wasn't, and it wasn't an overnight total transformation, but it did start with a decision.

A decision to a choice that became glaringly obvious after splitting up with my partner of 7 years. I was shaken to my very core as I became a single mother, solely responsible financially and in a business I'd lost all passion for AGAIN! I was stunned and numb from the reality as I knew it was ripped away.

Inside my head I had this little voice of absolute truth that said, 'you have one life, you have one shot!'

The voice continued, 'maybe it's time you didn't give failure the option to exist.'

There is one thing that I have been born with, and it's what I call GRIT. Grit is a determined positive attitude that keeps you running towards your dreams.

Through everything I have been through in my life, which is way too gory for this book, that grit has never gone away. But what I hadn't managed to do so far in the journey, was harness that grit. From the moment that little voice spoke, I was ready to become an oyster.

A new perspective was born. I was able to see that every failure and every stint of adversity was in fact a lesson that I could use to create success. It was time to turn that grit, both in the form of determination and harsh lessons, into a highly valuable, one of a kind pearl!

I realised the success and failure of my future was entirely within my control. I was faced with a glaringly obvious choice... continue to live with fear controlling my every move and nothing will change, the same luke-warm life will occur. Or choose to transform that fear that had been weighing me down and live the life I wanted.

I'm sure you can guess the choice I made. From there, I started. One foot in front of the other, I started to create my pearl. I remembered the promise and commitment that I'd made to myself - failure was no longer an option. It wasn't perfect, but unique excellence never is. I used the grit and continued to transform myself every day!

You see, the reason we self-deprecate is all down to perspective and the fact that we are ignoring the greatness we hold. We hold success at arms-length because our bar is raised so high, everything feels like a failure in comparison. But when you appreciate what you have in this very moment, that what you have *is* highly valuable to someone else, you find that you were sitting on a precious, one of a kind pearl all along.

Harnessing Grit

'It takes courage to grow up and become who you really are.' E.E Cummings

Courage… we ALL have it, we just have to learn to summon it.

That usually means holding your breath, not thinking too hard about it and taking a scary ass action!

If you think about it for too long, you'll be talking yourself out of it. Your brain will come up with all the possible scary negative outcomes and you'll 'sit on it' until you're ready. The truth is, you'll never be ready. Every decision, every step forward comes with it's consequences, good and bad. But the motivation for taking those steps usually come from a huge visible benefit to ourselves and others, which should far outweigh the negatives. The longer you stall, the longer you'll have to convince yourself it's a bad idea. Any decision (other than jumping out of the way of death), made through fear, will only lead you to a bad place or stuck right where you are.

'Taking action' is the badass version of making a decision. Taking action means you're committed. It means you're all in. It means there's no backing out. A decision without action can be unmade just as quickly as it was decided. From now on, make decisions through taking action, only then will you see true change and progress.

Nothing worthwhile doing is ever easy. A progressive action will be scary, it should be scary because if it's not scary you're not growing and if you're not growing, you're dying. It takes courage to BE yourself. Action speaks louder than words - yes that old chestnut. But it's true, action really does speak louder than words and so it's important to realise that to truly BE THE BEST VERSION OF YOU, it's not through just deciding who you want to be, it's about taking the actions that are aligned to be that best version of yourself.

This is going to be a cold hard slap in the face, but you need to realise that if you were already the best version of you right now, you'd be enlightened on some other plane having achieved everything you wanted to do, have and be already. Being the best version of you is an on-going process.

Action

- Decide who you want to be and write out all the things that this version of you does and does not do. The 'not do' part is just as important as the 'do'.
- What do you no longer tolerate from yourself anymore?
- What bullshit are you telling yourself on a daily basis that is holding you back from being that best version?
- Is this best version of you - wealthy, healthy, loving, in-tune, aligned, on purpose, kind?
- The list can go on and on, but what actions, behaviours and qualities can you take on right now to become that person you want to be.
- How is the current version of you, holding you back?
- Are you living and taking action through fear? Are you sabotaging through fear of failure, or even success?

Spend some real time on this. The key to your success really does lie in WHO you are. Your identity and your actions will directly impact the rest of your future success.

2

BELIEVE IN YOU

"Risk does not apply to those who believe in themselves." Jen Hall

'Who am I to do this?'

"Our deepest fear is not that we are inadequate. Our deepest fear is that we are powerful beyond measure. It is our light, not our darkness that most frightens us. We ask ourselves, 'Who am I to be brilliant, gorgeous, talented, fabulous?' Actually, who are you not to be? You are a child of God. Your playing small does not serve the world. There is nothing enlightened about shrinking so that other people won't feel insecure around you. We are all meant to shine, as children do. We were born to make manifest the glory of God that is within us. It's not just in some of us; it's in everyone. And as we let our own light shine, we unconsciously give other people permission to do the same. As we are liberated from our own fear, our presence automatically liberates others." Marianne Williamson

Who are you not to do this? You are just as worthy as the next person to step into the role of an expert and receive the success and abundance that you are entitled to. I'll say that again, it is your birth right to be here and serve others with your unique value... and you really are uniquely valuable!

We are great at taking ourselves for granted. We take for

granted what we know, our skills, the gift of our personality, our experiences, our successes, the lessons from our failures and the impact that we make on a daily basis. Yes, you heard right, the impact we make on a *daily* basis, because we all do, it may be on a small scale but we all have the potential and ability to make the world a better place and create a powerful a change in someone. And most of us do that everyday in the circles we hang around in. If you're reading this book it's highly likely you are an impact maker, because the kind of person this book attracts, already has an innate desire to impact people one way or another and can't help themselves when it comes to adding their value.

"Whether you think you can, or you think you can't—you're right." Henry Ford

After my sister had experienced a life changing event, she found herself sleeping on my sofa and at the time she was feeling pretty low. She had low self-esteem and low self-confidence largely to do with her previous relationship and felt like she was starting life all over again. But still, she was determined to stand on her own two feet again. Every day she'd wake up and hit the laptop to search for jobs and in the beginning, she was scouring for coffee shop roles, cleaning and retail assistant roles.

Now don't get me wrong, there is absolutely nothing wrong with anyone who works in either role, but you see the reason she was searching for those roles was because she felt like that was *all* she was capable of doing. She wasn't willing to look at anything over minimum wage because she didn't think that anyone would be willing to pay any more than that.

Each day she'd find a job description, open up her CV, and as any great CV should be, she started to tailor it to each job that she applied for. This meant she had to rewrite quite a bit of it (all true stuff) but she had to come up with examples for each of the things the job description was asking for.CV number one was complete, and she felt accomplished and off she sent it. CV two complete, and she started to build momentum… no responses back thus far but she was taking action and she was starting to feel those feelings of hope that life was about to get better.

What she and I started to notice though, was that after each application she started to gain more and more self-belief and self-worth because she was continually being asked to demonstrate how amazing she was, and she *had* to come up with the goods. She was forced to look at all the treasure that she'd been denying existed.

After application ten, she started to realise that she could do so much more than she first anticipated, and actually turned down a job offer at a coffee shop and another role with the utter belief that she had more to give which was worth way more than any of those jobs were offering.

She started to apply for higher paying roles which demanded more skill and after over 30 job applications, a few interviews, digging up her treasure on a daily basis and blowing her own trumpet, she landed a job at reputable organisation on more money than she ever thought possible, doing things that she'd always thought she couldn't do or was too scared to attempt.

All because she celebrated her greatness!

Make time to celebrate your wins and blow your own trumpet.

"Attract what you expect, reflect what you desire, become what you respect, mirror what you admire."

Action

- Pick someone you admire that you aspire to be 'like'.

- Now write out their 'job' description including responsibilities and person specification.
- Now apply for it by creating your CV to demonstrate why you're the best person for the job!

You'll soon see that you have way more GOLD than you give yourself credit for!

3

Positive Action

"Success seems to be connected with action. Successful people keep moving. They make mistakes, but they don't quit."
-- Conrad Hilton

My sister never could have got to where she is today without starting where she was at the beginning. In fact, it's true to say that for every successful person, they had to start where they were. Don't compare your first step or hundredth step to someone's ten thousandth. You must take action steps from where you are to get to where you want to go. You don't need to see the entire road, you only need to see the next few hundred yards.

Progress is so important to good vibes. When we're a place of good vibration, our energy is at a peak level for achieving the amazing goals we've set. If you're not feeling good, our belief in the ability to achieve those goals will be low and as I explained earlier, when we don't believe we create a self fulfilling prophecy of failure.

When we make progress our brain secretes dopamine, which is connected to pleasure, learning and motivation. It makes us feel good to move forward and achieve. In order to build momentum and make progress, it's important to take *consistent* action to achieve smaller goals.

It's no good deciding with words, words can be undone just as quickly as you spoke them. You must decide with committed action, that way you'll be making progress. Even if progress feels slow, forward is still forward.

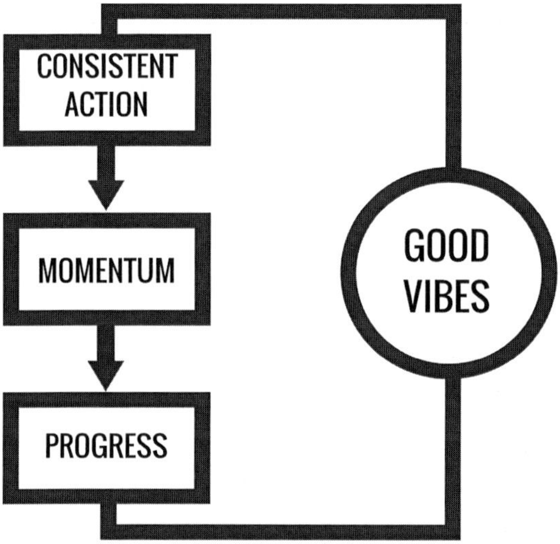

Good Vibes Equation

Fear of Failure

"Don't fear failure, fear being in the exact same place next year as you are today!"

Coca- Cola only sold 25 bottles in its first year. Colonel Sanders the founder of KFC, was a man who started at the age of 65 and failed 1009 times before succeeding. Star Wars very nearly didn't happen as it was turned down by several producers who didn't like the idea. Edison failed 1000 times before making the light bulb discovery. The stories are endless, but the lesson here is (if this hasn't already been hammered home), the only failure in this life is the failure to keep trying.

Around 15 years ago the term 'coach' was introduced to me. For a long time as a teen I wanted to be a counsellor, until I realised the main focus of the sessions were listening and helping to rectify the past for the person involved. This was a massive turn off for me as I had an innate desire to help people find their life purpose and that just wasn't appropriate in that field. So, when I heard about coaching, it was like my whole world lit up! I got excited, I was totally buzzed by the idea that I could help shape someone's future. So, I ordered a life coaching book and the day it arrived was the day I delayed my own life's purpose.

I opened the book and excitedly leafed through it, but as each page was reviewed a huge fear started to knot in my chest. 'I can't do this! This is all too complicated! I just wanted to help people and now it's going into all this NLP (neuro linguistic programming) stuff, that yes looks interesting, but I could never be trusted. This looks more like psychology than coaching!' and so I put the book on the shelf, never to be read fully again.

This is what my fear of failure looked like 'I'm not good enough,' 'People are going to laugh,' 'no one would ever trust me enough to help them, let alone pay me to help them.'

10 years went by with a varied career but with a bulk of it being in the recruitment industry (funny how looking back now I can see the link with life purpose), and a series of failed businesses under my belt. Year after year, repeating the same lukewarm patterns through fear of taking the steps to truly live my purpose, doing things that only half satisfied my hunger to help people.

The crunch point came when a 7-year relationship ended, and I became a single mum for the first time. I was suddenly solely financially responsible for our family of two and the stark cold truth hit me like a tonne of bricks. 'You cannot carry on like this!' I had been 'faffing about' for far too long and by this time I'd given up the corporate world to be an entrepreneur and the thought of going back to a job or carrying on in the business that only had one toe dipped in coaching when truly I wanted to become known as a COACH wholly and fully, was just not an option anymore. I rebelled and the desire to become what I always dreamed of being became so strong it was impossible for me not to take massive action towards it. Suddenly, any risk was worth it. Suddenly, I was willing to do what ever it took, no matter what. I decided with action, and invested in help to get me on the road to success. Once I truly opened my eyes to what was possible I realised success was assured if I kept trying and that I didn't care what others said or thought.

As soon as that decision was made I was locked in, there was no going back. Two months later after having taken that action, momentum started to build, and I realised something utterly life changing.

"Don't wait for opportunity, create it."

All this time I had been trying to fit myself into a box and nothing quite fit. Society and schools play a huge role in creating this mindset; anything outside the box is wrong and unacceptable. I wanted to class myself as something like a 'counsellor' or 'life coach' and those labels just didn't fit. I had no interest in NLP nor fixing childhood relationships. I was all about massive action towards your dreams and that just felt so 'wrong' in terms of what would be accepted by the world.

But I realised that I could create my own role. These days I use the word Coach but I'm by no means a coach in the traditional sense. My work includes mentorship, consultancy AND coaching. People are truly only interested in you solving their problems. How you do it, is really by the by; if you can help them get to where they want to go then stick two fingers up to traditional!

And that's exactly what I did. Through the process of using MY way, MY skills, MY experience, MY purpose I was able to chuck a large proportion of fear of failure to the dump. Trying to live up to someone else's version of what's 'right' will always leave you feeling like a failure.

After years of procrastination on taking action, I made rapid success! In just a year I had uncovered my value, owned it and positioned myself as a trusted expert as a Niche Coach, helping people to align their life's purpose with a money making niche and perfect ideal client to monetise their desire to impact the world.

You've got to be hungry for what you want. Make your desire bigger than your fears and you'll find taking that action that much easier.

Action

- What is the impact of stepping into the shoes of who you want to become?
- What is the impact for you and your family?
- What is the impact for the people you serve?
- Why is doing this so important to you?
- What are the consequences of NOT stepping into the shoes of the future you?

Success is Yours for the Taking

"The ones who are crazy enough to think they can change the world, are the ones who do."
Steve Jobs

Belief in what is possible for you is essential for you to achieve it. There is no strategy that can take you there without belief.

The best way to create belief in the possibility of 'unbelievable' success is to seek out real life stories of success built from adversity or so called 'nothingness' Every time I hear a story of rags to riches it immediately builds me up with excitement. It's almost like hope, but it's more than that, it's certainty that I too can achieve the same success.

I cast out long ago this belief that success is only available to the lucky. Because luck really isn't real, it's all cause and effect. You might not have complete control over external events, but you absolutely have control over how you respond to them and the actions you choose to take in this life.

There is no 'worthy stamp' for the chosen few who were deemed worthy enough for success. When you turn your dream into a plan and you commit to take action on that plan you are more than capable of achieving that dream.

My coaches have all been complete inspirations to me as they tell me stories of the mindset and financial state they were in and where they've come to. One of my mentors and coaches, Jessica Lorimer is one of those inspirations. She told me this story when I was at the beginning of my journey to creating the financial success I longed for. She told me the tale of how she left corporate to live her dream as an online entrepreneur helping people with her passion for sales, and 3 months in she was on the phone to her mother crying about how it's just not working out. Her very wise mother responded with the following:- 'When you first decided to do this you told me all the stories of the many before you who had created this successful laptop lifestyle making their millions as online entrepreneurs, so, what makes you so special to think that you can't do the same?'.

That story will forever stay with me and will serve a as a constant reminder that if someone else can do it, there is no reason why you can't.

For so long it was said that running a mile in 4 minutes was impossible, until the infamous Roger Bannister broke the record and managed to achieve the so called impossible. Since breaking that 4-minute barrier, several people have since achieved it as well. All because they were shown that it could be done.

"If my mind can conceive it, and my heart can believe it - then I can achieve it."

-- *Muhammad Ali*

Start by trying to achieve the smaller goals that lead you towards the BHAG (big hairy audacious goal). This will help to show you that you truly have control over achievement and as you build steam, make it your goal to break your own version of the 4-minute mile and inspire the world.

Belief is a choice. You either believe or you don't. There is no half way. Without belief in the possibility and in your ability to achieve, there is no success.

The reality is you probably don't have everything you need right to make the kind of success you want to achieve in the long term, no one ever does. But what do have is the ability to learn and grow. Never forget that. Keep on learning and keep on growing from the successes and the failures, because within every failure is a great lesson. Failure is not the opposite of success, it is part of it. As one of my favourite Business Coach's says, 'Welcome failure into your business, as it's through failure that you find success.' – Robin Waite

I'd like to add to that and say, mistakes are also how you

hone your expertise. So, don't avoid them, welcome them; it's all grit for your oyster.

The Unknown Consequence of 'Comparisonitis'

Comparison is not the thief of all joy as Roosevelt suggests, 'comparisonitis' is. The act of comparison as I've explained in the last chapter can be used to great lengths to boost your belief in the possibility, belief in yourself and can help you on your path, but 'comparisonitis' is a horrible curse of the mind where by you look at others and feel disappointed about where we are in relation to someone else's success level. That truly is the thief of joy and success.

To be truly successful, you must keep that passionate fire burning strong or this horrible disease of the mind will quickly dim that fire.

"Stay in your lane, there is less traffic and no speed limit"

In 1903 the Wright Brothers, Wilbur and Orville, successfully flew a 'heavier-than-air' plane on a sustained flight for the first time. But they weren't the only ones to be attempting to take flight. At the same time as their trials, Glenn Curtiss was also trying to build a flying machine, but unlike the Wright Brothers, he was heavily backed with finance and press coverage.

Sadly for Curtiss, this backing clearly didn't help him to be the first to fly, and on the on the 17th December 1903, the Wright brothers made a successful flight for the first time in history.

The Wright Brothers could have easily not bothered to try. They could have done what I did. At the age of 8 I gave up learning the violin when I'd only just begun because I made the assumption that I could never be as good as my sister so there was no point trying to compete. At that age I was so consumed with being 'better' that I missed the point of the whole thing.

The Wrights could have just as easily not tried and assumed that Curtiss had more of a head start, more resources and a better chance than they did. But they didn't, they stayed in 'their lane'.

It's worth noting, that whilst the Wright brothers were the first in many respects, Curtiss was the one who actually advanced the science and technology of human flight way beyond what the Wright's finally accomplished.

In 1929 Wrights' and Curtiss's organisations collaborated and merged to collaborate and combine their unique excellence and form the Curtiss-Wright Corporation.

As experts who want to be the best we can be, we must stay in our lane. We must not compare where we are to those who have already achieved great accomplishments. The best way you can achieve what you want to do is by drawing inspiration and keep your eyes on where you're headed.

Who knows where I'd be today if I'd stuck with the violin. Who knows of the many unfulfilled accomplishments that haven't taken place because of people who stopped because they felt hopeless in the shadow of their competitors and peers.

When you know how truly unique and valuable you are, there is no such thing as competition. You are truly unrivalled and powerful collaboration can be achieved.

Stay focused on creating your own unique pearl, when you copy through fear you end up with a cheap fake version which will never stand the test of time.

As you continue to move through this book, you'll gain more clarity on what makes you truly unique and with clarity comes confidence. All that is required is that you take courage to open the lid, discover what's inside, own it and show it off!

Fear of Playing Big & Growing

"If you want to be the anomaly, you need to act like one."
-- Gary Vaynerchuck

"In this world you're either growing or you're dying so get in motion and grow."

-- Lou Holtz

If you want great things, you must do great things, and great things mean scary action taking. But with scary action taking comes huge growth. When it gets scary, remind yourself why you're doing what you're doing. Make your purpose bigger than you and taking that action won't be so hard.

My mum used to say to me when I was child 'wouldn't it be nice to have a mansion, but think of all those rooms you'd have to clean!', I'd nod furiously and agree that it was a bad idea as the thought of having to help my mum clean as a child was more than I could bear. It was only as I got older that the penny dropped... if I could afford to buy a mansion, I could certainly afford a cleaner!

A lot of people have a fear of growing bigger. The unknown is scary as hell and I won't pretend otherwise, but you must remember that growing bigger means more revenue, more revenue means more capability and support. There is always someone out there to help guide you through the stages of growth. Yes, it means investment, but if you're a serious business owner, investing in your business is a MUST.

You don't need to see the whole journey, just the next step.

4

How much?

The first step in charging your worth is stop selling time for money. With time for money there is always a glass ceiling on how much you can earn, not only that, but your clients will be checking their watch and wanting results in as a quick a time as possible rather than focusing on the tasks at hand.

If you're not already doing so, switch to charging for the result, which means packaging up our services into a product. When we make this shift, we start to look at what we offer in a whole new light. We start to see the return on invest and value to the customer much clearer. When we know the value of what we offer it makes charging our worth that much easier.

One of my coaches, Jessica Lorimer introduced me to this analogy of the plumber which perfectly highlights how we should be charging.

"Amanda has an uncontrollable leak happening inside of her house and she calls an emergency expert plumber to come and sort it. Very quickly the plumber turns up, looks around, finds the problem and uses his equipment to fix the leak in just a few minutes. She thanks him and tells him how thankful she is as he's saved her thousands on damage that could have been made

structurally on the house, let alone the damage to the furniture and her late grandma's dresser. She then asks how much she owes him. He replies with – '£2000.' She gasps and responds with 'that's such a lot and you've only been here a few minutes!' The plumber replies 'you're not paying me for the time it took me to fix the leak, you're paying me because I know where to fix the leak."

The plumber had expertise that saved this woman a significant amount money from potential damage, stress, inconvenience and the loss of priceless possessions way beyond the initial £2k outlay.

Don't charge for time and equally don't underestimate the impact that your expertise has on someone's life or business. It's your job to highlight to your prospects explicitly the return on investment and the consequences of not fixing their problems and not achieving their wanted outcome.

Charging your worth takes courage but it's important to note that you must know your worth and own it in equal measures. What I mean is, you must feel good about the amount with every fibre of your being. If you feel out of integrity offering your services at a certain price, you'll block the sales because it'll show in the way you offer it that you doubt your value.

Your net-worth will never be greater than your self-worth. In the following chapters you'll be getting clearer on the incredible value you hold and the return on investment for the client. Until then, just remember this, people who see cheap, will associate you with cheap. And what ever you charge now, be prepared to increase those rates as you own your worth and increase your experience and skill level.

Owning your worth isn't just about money, it's the level of confidence that you have in yourself and what you offer, that will help you to beam like the sun to stand out from the crowd.

INGREDIENT 2: PURPOSE

5

Turning Purpose into Profit

Your purpose is the second ingredient in creating your unique cocktail that makes up what you offer and who you offer it to. Purpose is the life blood of your business and the energy that allows you to attract the people you can help the most - your ideal clients. In this section, we will be looking at your unique story, purpose and mission.

It's my goal for this next part to unearth your core message that will run through the entirety of your business presence. Your core message is responsible for being a clear, understandable and simple message that acts like a beacon that shines out to attract your following.

We are going to dig deep, explore your purpose which will provide the foundation for your mission and message, and we'll also uproot the story behind the message. Your purpose and mission will most likely be similar to many others out there, however, it's the story behind your mission that will be totally unique to you and the message you deliver will be expressed in your own unique way.

A lot of clients ask 'what do I do with this information upon discovering it?' By completing the life's purpose task and the mission statement they will help to give clarity to discovering and communicating your niche succinctly in the next section. The story and the core message can be used combined to communicate your 'viral idea' with your audience.

A 'viral idea' is an idea that spreads like a cold. In order to reach more people, you need share an idea that is so strong people will want to tell their friends about it. Cultivating a viral idea will make your marketing efforts effortless, as more people do the 'work' for you.

The 'share' button is the most used button on the planet, we are hard wired to want to share information, but an idea worth sharing is one that's strong, that worms it's way into the minds of your market and causes a shift in thinking. An idea that doesn't have this ability, will fall flat and will certainly not be shared. As the wonderful Seth Godin puts it 'There is no shortage of remarkable ideas, what's missing is the will to execute them.' He also says, 'You can't have good ideas unless you're willing to generate a lot of bad ones.'

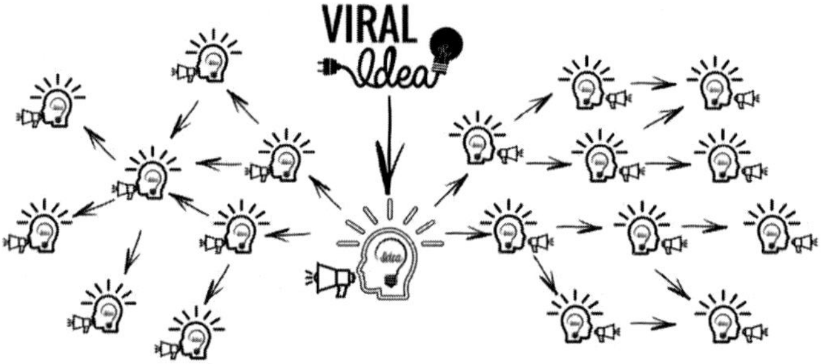

Your history, your story, your experience so far on this planet, and what drives you, will be plenty of inspiration to see a remarkably shareable idea come to fruition.

I want to mention again that clarity comes to people in a variety of ways; some people have to start at the beginning, others at the end and work their way back. If you find yourself struggling to complete the actions in this section or struggling to make sense of it, it might be worth moving to the next section and coming back to this one after. This section is laid out in the deliberate order to first discover your purpose, then your core message and then your mission. Working on your purpose and mission is the stepping to stone and foundation to discovering your niche, they'll also help to unearth your unique story which will connect with your following and run in congruence with your core message.

Everyone Has a Place on this Planet

Before we begin I want to bust a curse that has been with me for many years and I know it's also a curse that many others carry with them too. Brace yourself, because it's a strong one and if you hold this belief/feeling then I have some strong words for you...

'I feel like I bother people just by being alive.'

I'm sad to say, but this is something I truly believed for such a long time. I believed on a very strong level that I was more of a nuisance than I was help, which is part of the reason for my delay into stepping into my own purpose.

If this is something that just tugged your heart strings because you know this belief too, then it's time to let that shit go. It's one thing to feel like you have no purpose, which is the cause of much depression in this world, and another to think that you're 'in the way'.

This gut wrenching belief is something that I am passionate about breaking. We are all worthy human beings and we all have the ability to make the world a better place when your actions come from a place of love and integrity. So, go and live your life unapologetically. Take your rightful place in this world and go make the impact you were born to make.

You are here for a very important reason, you have a job to do, a purpose to fulfil and by not stepping up to that purpose, people are a heck of a lot worse off for it.

"There is no greater gift you can give or receive than to honour your calling. It is why you were born and how you become most truly alive"

-- Oprah Winfrey

Every moment is a gift and if we live each one to its fullest, acknowledge its beauty and its lessons, with the knowledge that each one is pregnant with the millions of possibilities for the future depending on how we choose to spend this one, our lives will become that much more exciting and beautiful.

Your purpose is your calling that ultimately forms your mission. It's your 'passionate why' that is way bigger than you. It's your contribution to the world that fills your soul and impacts the lives of others.

Your mission is the rocket fuel behind your business. It's what fires you up each and every day to reach beyond your perceived limits to make a difference. It's important for you and it's important in building your tribe and monetising your value.

In the words of the great Simon Sinek 'People don't buy what you do, they buy why you do it'. For me this isn't the only part of the buying picture, but it's certainly true that your world views and 'passionate why' forms a huge part of your overall brand, unique stance, and forms a calling for you to build a tribe of raving fans.

6

Discovering Your Purpose

In this next section, I am going to help you discover your life's purpose or at least gain clarity on what your purpose looks like. It's time to create a vision that's big enough to ignite the passion within. This will be the first step in discovering your mission which will then form as a foundation for creating your micro- niche.

Where there's passion and excitement in line with your mission and purpose, money and fuzzy warm feelings are sure to follow. It's about living to your full potential, being the greatest version of yourself and sharing your unique gifts with the world. When you work in this manner you can skyrocket your impact.

As you complete this section, it may be beneficial to park any preconceived ideas to one side. It's important that you follow your own purpose rather than someone else's. That doesn't mean that your purpose won't be similar to someone else's, what I'm saying is, don't follow something just because you think you should. It should be a true calling, something that is burning inside of you that you are genuinely passionate about.

THINK BIG, explore without preconceived limitations.

You serve no one playing small.

"The two most important days of your life are the day you were born and the day you find out why."

Limitation only lives in the walls we create for ourselves in our minds. Work with what you love, what you want, what sets you on fire, NOT what you think your purpose *should* be. This process should be fun and free flowing.

I'm going to show you a few ways to bring your life's purpose alive, so read the questions and write down your answers in as much detail as possible. If anything doesn't 'feel' right, just revise the answers until it's something that feels good to you. When it comes to your life's purpose statement you should feel content and happy with it. When we work on finding your micro- niche later in this book, you will feel aligned, excited, and a ton of brilliant ideas will usually flood in.

This exercise is an adaptation of an activity found in The Success Principles by Jack Canfield and it's one I've found extremely useful for both myself and my clients.

Ready? Let's go!

Action

- Write down 5 unique traits/personal qualities. Tip: If you're stuck, google positive personality traits and see what makes most sense to you!
- Pick 2 that resonate with you the most!
- Write down one or two ways you enjoy expressing those qualities when interacting with other people. For example: My qualities are MOTIVATIONAL & COURAGEOUS. I would state that I want women to do what excites them, so I encourage/motivate and

courageously lead by example through making those bold moves towards what brings me alive.

- What would your perfect world look like? For example: Mine is everyone would be doing what they loved, making the money they desired and helping each other by sharing their unique gifts with one another.
- Now let's put it all together to define your life's purpose... Mine is: "My life's purpose is to inspire and motivate people to live their life's purpose and make an abundance of money whilst doing so, by courageously leading by example, and empowering them with the tools to achieve their own dreams, and enabling them to share their gifts with the world!"

As you can see there is some creative licence here to make it something that truly resonates and means something to you. You will find after putting it together it might not make complete sense to you, so feel free to amend as you see fit to something that makes you feel happy and content.

- **Now write yours...**

Now you've created your statement you will have the basics there, but I'd like you to answer the following questions as well. This may or may not provide you with additional insights that you can tweak the statement so that you feel truly happy with it. There are no hard and fast rules.

Here are some more mind jogging questions to help you uncover your purpose...

- **What did you want to 'BE' / 'DO' when you were growing up?** Look at the reasons behind why; what was it specifically about these vocations that made you want them? So, for instance, I wanted to be an

Actress because I liked influencing people with a moral message and working with an audience. I also wanted to be an Art Teacher, so that I could enable others to express themselves in non conformative ways and be proud of their achievements whilst expressing my own creativity. Today, I influence people by motivating them to live limitlessly with passion in non conformative ways.

- **What makes you feel alive?**
- **What could you talk about for hours, where the words just fly out your mouth?**
- **What brings you absolute joy?**
- **What's your Personal Power?** What skills, experience & knowledge do you bring to the table? Think about your experiences: Jobs / Careers / Industries, Courses Attended/Qualifications, Life Experience, Other careers you've wanted...

AHA!

So, knowing all this information, your purpose and your personal power and what excites you...

- **If you could create any role (that may not even exist at the moment) what would it be?**

Jot down some initial ideas for now, and we'll revisit and explore this in more depth later.

This exercise may have done one of two things...

1. Confirmed and strengthened the clarity on your purpose behind what you are currently doing and you

will likely feel more motivated than ever to get out there and fulfil your purpose!

2. You may have come to the realisation that what you were doing just isn't in alignment with your life's purpose and / or your passions. If this is the case, don't be disheartened, be grateful for the wake-up call. It is NEVER too late to act upon your life's purpose and walk your true path. Yes, it's scary, yes it means letting go of hard work, money and time invested BUT, would you rather continue to live a life unfulfilled or make the changes to make the most of your ONE life that you have been privileged to lead?

Whatever your life's purpose has inspired, it best be BIG, it must excite you, it must be a burning desire and it MUST SCARE THE SHIT OUT OF YOU!

No one ever made progress in their comfort zone! BELIEVE IN THE POSSIBILITY!

7

Your Core Message

A core message is a high-level message that will resonate and attract your tribe to build a following for your business. It will be closely linked to your 'passionate why,' purpose and what you deliver.

Of course, you may find that you have many other messages to pass on, but your core message is the ONE message that all other messages branch out from and it's usually related strongly with your chosen niche, and as such, I recommend revisiting this after you've completed section 3 'The Glass.'

Finding this message will form the core of what you're going to be known for, it will play a vital role in communicating a 'viral' idea. An idea and a message that will spread from one person to another, IF it's strong enough, IF it speaks to the hearts and minds of each person in your target market and IF it's unique and powerful enough to appear remarkable.

Your core message is actually easier to find than you first might think and that's exactly what we're going to uncover in this next section. The work you've done in the life's purpose section should help you answer these questions, but we'll start to get more focused and specific to then create your mission statement.

Before we begin I'd like to give you an example of some core messages that will help you understand what they look like.

- 'Be the BEST option in the marketplace by being YOU, the world ain't seen nothin' yet!'
- 'Sales shouldn't be sleazy, it's about selling with integrity'
- 'Losing weight doesn't mean eating 'boring' food'
- 'Choose love instead of needing love and break away from unhealthy relationships'
- 'Growing your bank balance doesn't mean you have to stop spending'
- 'You are not fat, you *have* fat, now let's get rid'

Let's get started...

Three Short Cut Questions

The quickest and easiest way to get to your why and core message is to answer these questions. (I have another task below to help jog your brain into action should you struggle to answer them so don't worry): -

1. **What is the transformation you want to see in the world and why?**

Try and be specific, if you write down 'to see everyone achieve their dreams' that's too generic; replace the word everyone with who you're really talking to and describe what the 'dream' actually looks like, because that will be different for everyone. When you write down why, start thinking back to stories that have led you to wanting others to experience the transformation and just make note of them for them for the moment.

2. **If you were asked to stand up in front of 100,000 people and share one message with them, what would you say?**

Bearing in mind you can choose the type of people in the audience...

- Who would they be?
- How would they be moved by your message (i.e. what action would it inspire them to take)
- And why is it so important to you to share it with them?

3. **If you could only teach one thing, what would it be and why?**

Dive Deeper into Your Core Message

It's all in the stories!

One BIG thing to remember when working out your why, is to realise that the gold is in the SMALL stories from your past, in the little things that MATTERED to you! It might not appear particularly monumental to others, but for you the epiphany may have happened in the tiniest of moments and in everyday ordinary living. Remember the gold is sometimes in the small stuff so don't disregard ANY story.

Also, remember that nothing has meaning except the meaning you give it, so your stories are incomparable to anyone else's. They are what they are, and they meant what they meant at the time.

When you complete the below task, write without judgement and accept them for the moments in time that they were and the significance they had on you regardless of anyone else's perception of them. This is not a time to criticise or compete with who has the biggest or best story... the GOLD is usually in the small and seemingly normal stuff.

If you struck gold from the shortcut questions it might be worth having these messages in mind when you begin writing, or you can attempt this from a blank space to try and jog the messages, it's entirely up to you.

- Get two pieces of blank paper and you're going to write down stories from your past that made the biggest impact in your life to date, these are usually some of the most memorable and can have arisen at any age.
- On the other sheet write down the stories that perhaps might be difficult to think about because they may have had a more negative impact. However, it's important to note that these events have still made a huge impact on you and they form part of who you are today. The most important thing to do now is to determine the positive lesson from each of those stories. We can learn from those moments, we don't have to be defined by them. Make sure you write down the *positive* lessons learned from those situations.
- Make sure that you're being as specific as possible about those memories/stories and write down how they made you feel, the details and what specifically about those moments impacted you the most.
- Once you have your stories, it's time to pull out the **common** lessons learned from those moments. If you're struggling to find a common thread, ask a trusted friend/colleague. It's important that they don't know you too well because I wouldn't want them to skew the perspective of your stories too much.

- Now you have your one common positive lesson that you'd want to share with the world, turn this lesson into a statement.
- Ask yourself how you'd like others to specifically take action on this message? What would you like to see them achieve in their lifetime using this message?

Your core message must be something that you feel truly passionate about and connected with. You need to be able to make it specific enough to help it make sense to the specific people who you are talking to. It is something that you should truly be excited for someone to take action on. When defining it, have this in mind... what do you want people (a particular type of person, not just everyone) to do with your message? What is the mindset you want them to cultivate? What action do you want them to take?

It might help to revisit the shortcut questions at this stage. We'll be revisiting your message in the last section, but for now let's move onto the final part of this section which will bring everything you've been working on so far in this section together.

8

Your Mission

It's time to create your mission statement. From working on your life's purpose and your core message you should have some more clarity to start getting more specific.

Your mission will get you closer to your micro-niche as much as you can be at this stage, but we'll cover micro-niching in much more detail in the next section following this one. Your mission forms the bridge between your purpose and your micro- niche.

Your mission statement will sound something like this...

"To.... so that..."

Example: To *(insert action & who)* empower ambitious entrepreneurs with the means to see their unique value so that *(insert outcome)* they can position themselves as the best option in the marketplace, make epic impact and earn an epic income.

Try and make your statement as specific as possible and try not use words that are too vague. It's fine to start vague, but drill it down. You might have to write this down a few times before you get it right. The next section will also help you to get more specific.

Your mission on its own won't ever be totally unique, because your mission is to inspire people to join you and support that mission. If your mission was totally unique and abnormal there would be no common desire to join you on your collaborative journey and inspire the people that you are here to help.

Remember it's the cocktail as a whole that will help you stand apart as the unrivalled expert.

Be Prepared for Shifts

It's worth noting that it may be helpful to revisit your stories and your core message once you've completed micro-niching in section 3. This is because from a marketing perspective you'll probably be able to dig up more relevant stories to the problems you solve and the outcomes you help your clients achieve that your prospects will resonate with.

The purpose of these exercises for the moment is to gain clarity on your why, your mission and your purpose. Clarity tends to shift and change very quickly; move with the process, trust it and as you revisit the sections, and through completing the exercises in this book you'll find increasing alignment to who you are, what you offer and your unique excellence. With that, you'll be able to better communicate this with your audience.

Don't fret if you notice things change, it's about finding a place in your heart and mind that feels aligned. Be prepared to let go of stories, redefine them and shift your focus so that you can find your unrivalled position in the coaching world.

Having purpose helps to obliterate fear. It's making what you do bigger than just you and your little world. It places a bigger responsibility to the action you take, because if you don't, the world will be missing out on the important impact you have to make. The potential impact that could be lost through fear on a daily basis is huge. It's easy to hold ourselves back because being visible feels vulnerable, because you're scared you'll be trolled or disagreed with. None of that really matters when you have a bigger job to do, the job of making a difference. The world is counting on you to be your best, so put on that bulletproof vest and be you!

INGREDIENT 3: THE GLASS

9

Choosing the Right Glass

To monetise your purpose and truly turn it into profit, it's important you pick the right glass to pour your cocktail into. In fact, the glass is a major part of your cocktail. It's not just any old glass, it's a special type of glass that entices you to drink the cocktail and *allows* you to drink it. It's the vehicle between what you want to deliver and your prospect being able to receive it. Beyond this metaphor I'm talking about your micro-niche.

Micro, although meaning small, is a powerful way to dominate your corner of the market. Finding your micro-niche makes up a significant proportion of your unique cocktail and done effectively will bring more alignment to you and your business than ever before. It will help you remove your fluffy and vague exterior and provide a laser sharp focus that will stand out from the saturation.

It's about getting specific on what you want to be known for. When I talk about your prospect being able to receive what you want to deliver, what I really mean by this is that you need your prospect to *want* to receive it. It's about packaging it up in a way that's desirable and makes sense to them to invest in what you're offering.

What is a niche and what is a micro-niche?

- A niche is a group of people who share a common problem.
- A micro-niche is a group of people who you can label, who all share a specific problem and a specific shared desire.

To stand out of the saturation and position yourself as an expert in your field, finding your micro-niche is imperative.

No one wants to work with a jack of all trades. People want to work with someone who specialises in solving their specific problem to help them achieve their specific goals. You can't be all things to all people, that is the exact opposite of an expert.

Picking a large group of people who share a large-scale problem isn't going to help you stand out, you'll just join the rest of the pens in the 99p pen pot. You need to go three layers deep to position yourself effectively and I'll be showing you how to do that in the following chapters.

A lot of people think that just by naming a group of specific people will be enough to attract clients and position them as the expert, but that's not how it works. People want to know what you help them with specifically and what that means to them. So yes, the 'who' is important for giving your solutions context but it's imperative that we nail the other two pieces of the puzzle to truly find direction and be certain we have a wanted service.

When you don't niche these things happen: -

- You appear as a 'jack of all trades' with no specialism and diluted skills.
- Marketing becomes vague as you try and communicate many different solutions to many different people,

resulting in a lack of connection with your audience.

- You can become disconnected with your 'passionate why,' the real reason you decided to do what you're doing. This will come through energetically in everything you do, and you will gradually lose steam.
- Telling people what you do is hard work, and your audience can get confused about whether you can help them or not. Confused minds don't buy.

When you decide to micro-niche, this happens: -

- You become an expert in your field and build trust with your audience.
- You pull yourself apart from the competition and take a unique stance.
- You can get really specific about who your ideal client is, making your marketing hugely effective and targeted.
- Your communication about you and your business becomes super easy.
- You know what opportunities are right for your business and what isn't!
- You become aligned with your passionate why, and your message, story and mission shines through in your communication.
- Your ideal client knows that you can help them with their specific problem or need, making you truly desirable.
- Referrals become a regular thing as people know who you are, what you specialise in and who to refer to you.
- If that isn't enough to convince you that micro-niching is the route to success, then try this for size. When you

micro-niche, it not only improves your marketing, positions you as an expert, makes writing content, creating packages and products that sell super easy, it's all because you're in alignment with your passion and purpose. Imagine waking up every day with that excitement and fire in your belly to fulfil your purpose and mission. To know that what you are doing that day will change someone's life.

Micro-niching was something way back in the beginning I knew I needed to do but found so hard nail down.

Reason being? I focused too much on what I thought I 'should' be doing rather than what I wanted. I was so distracted, I failed to see what I was amazing at doing and what I was truly inspired to help with. I was also scared!

If I'm going to get really honest with you, I'll also admit that I was scared of cutting out the market and potentially picking the wrong niche. The reality is, the niche I chose at the beginning has far evolved past recognisability. It started out niched, not micro-niched and it's changed shape gradually as I've embraced the powerful process of focusing in.

I know that without micro-niching effectively I wouldn't be here writing to you about it today. I would still be struggling to try to help people who didn't want to be helped and with things I'm really not made to help with.

10

Niche Fear

The Fear of Niching

A lot of people will talk about niching being too hard because they are multi passionate and it's impossible to choose just one area. They'll claim they don't want to because it doesn't feel 'good' to. But here's the cold hard truth, if you don't pick, you'll be in for a world of struggle! It's literally a choice between struggle or success... pick from those options and suddenly the choice becomes a lot easier.

Many people fear niching for a few reasons, which I'll tackle now.

1. **Fear of cutting out the market and not gaining enough clients.**

So firstly, something that a mentor once said to me: - 'Everyone is no one in business.' It was the first seed that was ever planted in my head that opened my eyes to a lot of the failure that I had experienced in previous businesses. To be heard, you must speak to someone.

Ever tried explaining the value of something you're super passionate about to your family and they just didn't 'get it'?

That's because everyone is different. We all have different priorities, opinions on what's important in life, different wants, different problems, different values etc. To assume everyone needs or wants your product is an ignorant view indeed, and one that will fall on deaf ears.

It may seem counter intuitive but by being specific you'll be heard by more people, and client attraction will become a much easier process.

2. **Fear of having to get specific because they're too scared to claim they can achieve specific results or the results people truly desire.**

Staying in integrity with the results you claim to be able to give people is crucial to your confidence, your positive energy, your mindset and successfully converting prospects into clients. What you must realise, is that you can't cover every eventuality for your client and that there are many ways to peel an orange. It's your job to OWN your way as the greatest way to achieving the outcome. You will be responsible for providing a puzzle piece that they need to achieve the result the client wants.

For instance, I help to position coaches and consultants as experts in their field. I do that by helping them find their unique selling proposition, micro-niche, alignment and confidence. But there are others out there who get he same result, but they do that through PR, writing a kick-ass book or becoming a great public speaker.

You have to sell people what they want and sometimes that may involve talking about a scarily big outcome like making money, losing weight or finding the man of their dreams. Saying this may feel scary because we worry that our clients might not achieve the outcome.

There's a couple of things to mention here.

- You are providing a puzzle piece to that wanted outcome, yes it may not be the only puzzle piece that they require, but you do know that without your puzzle piece that you hold they will not achieve the outcome at all.
- The next thing to mention is that you cannot take 100% responsibility for the result. Your clients play a huge part in implementing the coaching and the tasks they get set. You can give someone the finest mop but unless they are willing to use it, their floor will remain dirty. Before you take any money from them, make them aware of the part they play in achieving the results and be honest with them about managing their expectations. Be confident in what you provide but depending on their current state of play and willingness to grow it will impact the level of results they can achieve. You can make sure your contracts are developed with these expectations written in.

A powerful statement to bear in mind whilst working through this section is, whatever it is that you're too scared to promise your clients as a result, that's your money-making result. If you're too scared to promise a result to them, it's likely that's it's a very desirable outcome and you'd have to be pretty bold to promise it, if you catch my drift.

3. **Fear of picking the 'wrong' thing and not being able to change their mind.**

Let me set the story straight right now on this one. You can change your mind at ANY point. It's your life and you have the right to choose what happens next.

Obviously changing your mind comes with consequences and the more you chop and change your niche, particularly before you've embedded it, will put you back to the beginning again in terms of making a big dent and becoming known for the new thing you've chosen. However, if you choose something that isn't aligned then it's vital that you change so you can find your passion.

What you need to know is that when you follow passion your decision will never be wrong. Your decision does not need to be forever, but you do need to stick a stake in the ground and decide.

Once you've decided, the doing becomes effortless and progress follows very quickly. Choosing not to decide, will keep you in no mans land and will delay your success.

11

How to Pick the Right Niche

There is a danger of picking the wrong thing from the outset and I want to help you cross these things off the list to save you getting in a pickle further down the road.

What you need to be prepared to do, is let go of the 'shoulds' and the investment you've already made into a direction you've been taking already. Yes, you may have spent years studying for it, you may have invested plenty of $$$ into it, you may have a lot experience or skills in that area, BUT if you don't love it, if it isn't an obsession, if it doesn't bring you alive, you'll never make any money and you'll lose steam! It will be a hard slog.

Don't work in a niche you hate, or 'choose' an audience you don't really want to work with because you think it will be easier to gain clients. You'll resent your business if you work in that manner.

Let go of the attachment to the fact you think you have a duty to work in a certain area because of the knowledge and expertise you currently have to date.

You have the ability to learn new things. We only get one life so let's stop doing the things that turn us off and start doing the things that light us up. We are people of many talents and we are a treasure chest full of amazingness to choose from that can transfer over into various niches.

What you will find in general though, is that the things you have *chosen* to do in the past will most likely be in alignment to your life's purpose, don't discount your history.

The biggest challenge you have in marketing yourself is simply getting people to stop and notice you. Once you've got their attention you have the amazing opportunity to give them free value, build trust and help them make a huge transformation with your paid products.

To get people to listen to you, they need to understand what's in it for them. Which is why the more specific you can get, the better, because you're able to make it absolutely clear if you're the right person to be listening to, or not. With all the noise of social media and the like, is it worth their precious time?

In the following steps, I outline how you can go about defining your micro-niche. Not by focusing solely on their pain points but by focusing on their aspirations and priorities as well. Use the clarity you found in section two to help point you in the right direction when going through these steps.

12

4 Step Method to Define Your Micro-Niche

Why People Buy

By following these steps you'll be tapping into the science behind why people buy. People buy in two stages, firstly 'emotionally' and secondly, they like to justify their decision to buy with logic. When you discover the prospects 'success island' you'll be tapping into the emotional desire to buy from you and when you cover the problem you solve and the solid outcome, you'll be aligning with the logic people need to justify their desire to buy from you. You need to tap into your clients desires both on an emotional level and a logically level to position yourself as irresistible in your field.

What's the transformation?

Showing people the transformation they will receive is the best way to convert your prospects as it builds a strong emotional connection from the outset.

To communicate the transformation effectively to your prospect, you will be describing the before and after state of what will happen to them once they have worked with you. This will be described as what they have, feel and their identity, both before and after working with you. A great way for you to gain clarity on how to effectively describe the transformation in your marketing is to write 'a day in the life of...' for both before and after. I also call this the Hell and Heaven exercise. Writing down what they're experiencing on these dramatically stark scenarios allows you to really tap into the emotions and the physical reality of the situation.

Before & After Transformation

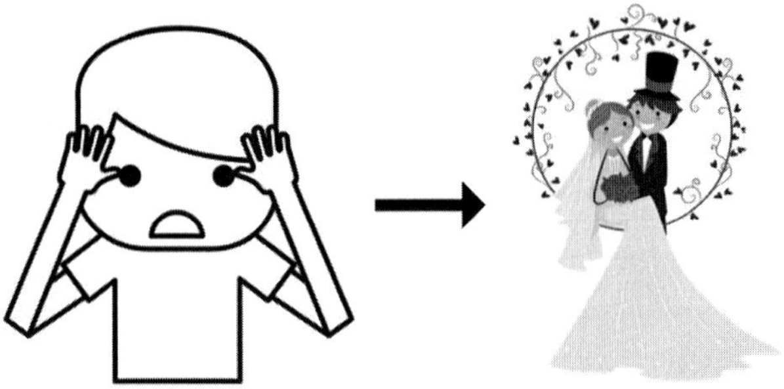

One of the most motivating drivers for people to truly want something from you, is to know 'who' they will become after they have worked with you. When you dangle the carrot of becoming that desired identity it will make a strong emotional connection to wanting to 'have' your solid outcome.

Think perfume ads. In every perfume ad there is a character of some sort that the marketers want you to desire. Whether that's the suave, suited man with the ladies, the rough and ready adventurer or for women the city woman who dares to be wild or the sweet country girl who's care free and flirty.

Whether you personally identify with these particular characters I've mentioned here or not, someone does, and it makes a significant difference to who's attracted to buy the product.

An Intriguing Experiment...

"Three randomized experiments found that subtle linguistic

cues have the power to increase voting and related behaviour. The phrasing of survey items was varied to frame voting either as the enactment of a personal identity (e.g., "being a voter") or as simply a behaviour (e.g., "voting"). As predicted, the personal-identity phrasing significantly increased interest in registering to vote (experiment 1) and, in two statewide elections in the United States, voter turnout as assessed by official state records (experiments 2 and 3). These results provide evidence that people are continually managing their self- concepts, seeking to assume or affirm valued personal identities. The results further demonstrate how this process can be channelled to motivate important socially relevant behaviour."

Source: Motivating voter turnout by invoking the self

In laymen's terms, the study examined the voting patterns of 133 adults to see if labelling them had any effect on their turnout to vote.

Half of the participants were told that they were much more likely to vote since they had been deemed by the researchers to be 'more politically active.' This wasn't true; these people were selected at random. The other half of the participants weren't told anything.

Despite this random selection, the group that was told they were "politically active" had a 15% higher turnout than the other group.

We all want to achieve a certain identity in this life or we want to be associated with a certain type of 'label' in order to feel good about ourselves and feel approved of. If we feel like it's going to improve our status and associate ourselves with a group of people that's respected or of 'superior' quality, then we're going to want to be a part of what you're offering so we can be 'approved' of.

The interesting thing is, our version of 'superior' or 'status' differs from person to person. Why do you buy certain clothes and not others?

Label the person that your ideal client wants to become and go a step further and label the person that your ideal client wants to move away from being.

Think about who you're helping your prospect become through providing your solid outcome.

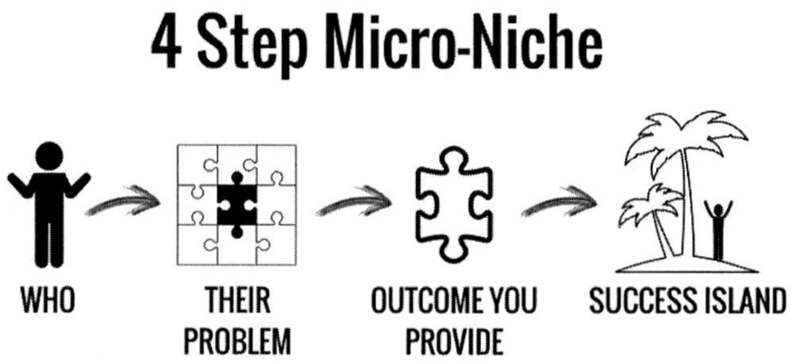

The diagram above will simplify the steps when looking at creating your micro-niche, but each of these steps are made up of further elements which I'll go through in more in detail.

A Great Example

To explain the process of micro-niching, I'm going to use examples from both my business, my clients, and of my partner Andy's business. These examples will show you very simply how you can apply the following four steps.

Here's a high overview of Andy's business journey to micro-niching...

Andy runs an adventure travel business and specialises in helping people reach Everest Based Camp. When he first started out 2 years ago he was a business who wanted to help *anyone* go on *any* adventure. He named his company Bucketlist Adventure Travel and created a website that hosted biking, fishing, rock climbing, trekking and many more things. He soon found himself overwhelmed with his marketing efforts and struggled to gain any serious traction.

Through some strong persuasion he agreed to start with *one* thing - the Everest Base Camp trek. He soon saw the rewards in the form of more people paying attention and spending money, and started to become known for helping people reach EBC. He became known as the company that used local guides and local companies to make sure as much money stays in Nepal as possible in order to rebuild the country following the devastating earthquakes. His true passion was in high altitude trekking in Nepal and realised the only reason he tried to offer so much was to try and serve as many people as possible. He found that by picking one thing, his marketing became slick and targeted. He rebranded six months ago and changed his business name to Evertrek, and is now on track to reach half a million in turnover in 2018.

Step 1 - Go deep!

A lot of people waiver on the edge of being specific but never fully take the plunge. For instance, a lot of Life Coaches, Health Coaches and Business Consultants try to help everyone with every problem in these VERY large markets. This leaves you liking a Jack of all trades and a master of none!

In reality, within these large markets there is a second and third layer that must be found in order to truly find an expert status and a money-making micro niche. In order to find that third layer, we must get really specific on the who. Not the 'who' in regards to a market of people, I'm talking about getting so specific we're talking about an individual person. It is each individual person that makes up a market that has the ability to be monetised. Give your 'who' a contextual label so that if the person were listening to you they could self identify with it. Labels could include female entrepreneurs, single mums, male diabetics. The key is that you define exactly WHO you are talking to at a micro level.

-For instance, a Health Coach could take it further to help people specifically with weight loss. But even then, the weight loss market is still pretty huge, so they should take that further and potentially dive into transformational weight loss specifically for people who suffer with under-active thyroids.

-In Andy's case, he went from targeting 'people who love the outdoors' to trekkers and hikers.

-In my case, instead of targeting business owners, I target Coaches, Consultants & Experts.

Step 2: What's the overall 'Success Island' that your ideal client wants to get to?

Your prospects success island is the ultimate goal they are trying to achieve. People only pay for what they truly value, so the 'success island' should speak to one important thing - their priority. If it's a true desired priority they will be willing to spend whatever it takes for the right help to achieve it.

To answer this question, ask...

- 'Who' does your ideal client want to be?
- How does your ideal client want to be perceived by the world?
- What do they want to achieve?
- Why is it a priority to my ideal client and why is it so important to them?

- What does it mean for them to reach their desired goals and status?

Be as specific as possible.

-Here's an example of my ideal client, my prospect wants to be a highly sought after, unrivalled expert who earns a high income.

-In Andy's case, his prospect has a dream of reaching Everest Base Camp, they want to complete a seriously hard challenge and be able to come home and tell their friends of the incredible adventure they had. They want to be known for doing extraordinary things. It's something that they aspire to achieve on the pursuit of completing the toughest challenges. They have a reputation as an adventurer to keep up!

-In the case of my client Niki, a Weight Loss Coach, her clients want to become confident, fit and thin so they can embrace the spotlight and visibility that their job demands them to have. They want to be that white-hot authority who feels fierce.

Step 3: What's the problem?

Without a problem to solve, you don't have a business. Getting really clear on who you're serving and selling to means you can get really clear on the genuine problem you're solving. People are different, and different sorts of people have different needs and different problems which is why it's so important to get specific. Your ideal client has to be aware of their problem, you shouldn't have to convince them of it. They are not going to want you to solve something that they're not feeling 'pain' from.

Whilst you might be solving an external problem, people are actually much more motivated to solve an internal problem. Solving the internal problem is what will convert your clients emotionally speaking, and as I mentioned earlier, people buy emotionally first.

- What problem is your ideal client experiencing that is preventing them from reaching their 'success island'?
- What is the external problem that you are solving?
- What is the internal problem that you solve?
- External Problem:- Andy's clients need someone to organise the trip and enable them to complete their 'challenge'

Internal Problem:- Andy solves the more pressing issue of peace of mind. They want to make sure their exciting trip is in the right hands so they can rest assured that everything is taken care of and that they'll be totally looked after with best Trekking Expert at their disposal to make sure they actually reach Base Camp and get their safely.

External Problem:- Jo, Public Speaking and Communications Expert, she works within corporate to help top execs and directors nail key note presentations and important internal speeches, ensuring they become structured, punchy and deliver more impact.

Internal Problem:- Jo actually solves critical confidence issues and helps to avoid potential change management failure and reputation damage for both the individual and the organisation as a whole.

- Why do you believe it important to overcome these problems?

People like to be part of something bigger than themselves or that speaks to their inner sentimental beliefs/world view.

For example:-

- Evertrek believes in making the seemingly unreachable reachable.
- Jo believes in Leaders who Lead with impact and authenticity.
- Niki, the Weight Loss Coach, doesn't believe you *are* fat, only that you *have* fat and it's something you can obliterate quicker and easier than you first imagine.

Step 4: How do you help them get to their 'Success Island'?

Whilst your transformation is vitally important, it's also important to be clear on your solid outcomes that get them to that transformation, and without writing a whole other book on just this topic, it's important to mention that people want to justify in their minds the money they are going to spend with you.

They will want to know how you're planning on helping them achieve that desired transformation. There will be something that they truly want that they think once they get it, will help them achieve the transformation they desire. This belief will be so strong that you'd be wasting your time trying to tell them otherwise. This why it's super important that you 'sell them what they want and give them what they need' I cover this in more detail in the next section.

Examples of solid outcomes and transformations could be:-

- Writing a Best-Selling book to become a respected expert.
- Gaining clarity on their USP and Micro-niche to become a stand out, go-to expert.
- Building a solid mindset around their relationship with

food to lose 2 stone and rock that little black dress at the Christmas do.

- Training to peak fitness and learning high-altitude trekking techniques to reach Everest Base Camp, completing a challenge and life long dream that will never be forgotten.

As much as we might want to invest, we're smart consumers and we want to know the plan of action!

- What wanted tangible solid outcome do you get for your client that will help them achieve their success island/ transformation?
- To ensure your outcome is solid, ask yourself how the client will measure their success, how will they know they've achieved what you are promising?
- 'How' do you help them overcome their problems? Do you have modalities, processes or techniques that you use specifically?
- What stages of success do you help people achieve that would get them to 'success island'?

For instance, the way I help my clients achieve the status of in-demand, unrivalled expert is through helping them gain clarity on their USP, niche, brand and building a solid mindset to truly 'feel' like a unique and invaluable expert who charges their worth. However, someone else might help them write a book to position themselves as the high-profile expert, or perhaps give them a PR plan to become more visible as the expert in the spot-light. Perhaps a mindset coach would focus on the psychology of the client's mind to help them understand their unique worth.

Defining the solid outcomes will help your prospect apply

logic and justify their decision to buy from you.

Recap! Do's and Don'ts of Micro-Niching

- Don't pick something just because it's popular or what you 'think' might sell the best. Your niche must be in alignment with what sets you on fire and your true zone of genius.
- Do remember that what you want to give and what someone will pay for is two very different things BUT they both must co-exist for the sake of it being a viable and enjoyable business.
- Don't think about your niche from your own perspective or focus on the process of how - this won't sell.
- Do think about it from your ideal client's perspective, this is the only way you'll create a niche that truly 'speaks' to people.
- Do find a place to start if you're struggling to piece together the steps, not everyone finds clarity in the same way. At the forefront of your mind you may have one of these that sticks out more obviously than the others - you may have a message that's important for someone to hear in order to achieve something, some of you may have a fierce mission that you want to help others also achieve, some of you may have a very valuable skill that you know can be hugely beneficial to someone.
- Don't confuse a niche with the 'who'. Whilst the who is very important to your marketing, simply naming a group of people like 'single mums' isn't a niche, it's the problem you solve, and the end result you help those people achieve that's the niche.

Check- In

- Who do you help? (Give them a label so they can self-identify)
- What's the ONE BIG thing you help them achieve?
- Who does that help them become?
- What's the ONE BIG problem you solve for them?
- Why is this important to them?
- Why is this important for the world?

Action

Create your 'Clear as Day' Niche Statement

This statement is a short set of words that clearly explain what you do and the transformation you provide in a concise and contextual manner.

Let me give you some examples: -

- 'I help budding dinner entertainers become pro's in the kitchen by teaching them the secrets of Top Chef's.'
- 'I help Coaches & Experts position themselves as the best option in the market place through micro-niching and uncovering their USP '
- 'I help Corporate Directors become Inspiring Authoritative Leaders through helping them hone effective and impactful communication skills.'

- ‘I help professional women who are done with the fat, to look and feel fab, fit and fierce.’

Now your turn to write yours...

INGREDIENT 4: MAGIC

13

The Truth About Magic

To be wanted by your ideal client you must have a unique, new and somewhat magical solution to their problem.

Claiming you are better at doing what other people do is just not going to cut it. Your prospects may already be hooked to someone else's solution and so trust is already built, and when someone has their trust, it's done, the only way to hook your prospects is to offer something NEW.

Busting the Myth

In the coaching and consulting industry we spend quite a lot of our time bleating on about magic pill hunters. What we are really trying to do is educate people that the overall outcome you're helping them achieve will not be achieved overnight and without doing the work necessary. But what happens is, we spend all our time fighting off these 'trouble making' potentials who truly don't want to do any of the work to achieve the result, is that we forget that we all have a desire on some level for someone to wave a magic wand and make everything better.

The difference between the 'trouble makers' and the ones who will do the work, is that if someone were to wave a magic wand and say, 'your wish is my command IF you do the following...' they would take that 'if' caveat like a shot. Whereas the 'trouble makers' can't be arsed. They're quite happy to let everything float into their lap without having to lift a finger.

We need to accept that to go fishing, we must have some kind of bait, and before we start the sorting process between the trouble making fish and the good ones, we must first catch the fish. This comes back to defining the big juicy outcome and transformation that you're helping the client achieve. But it's also about the new, shiny way that brings hope to the prospect that they can indeed achieve their ultimate goals.

For most people, they would have tried to solve the problems they have already, so they will have very likely tried to solve the problem themselves first and foremost and perhaps even invested in some kind of help already. The prospect needs to feel confident that it WILL work this time.

- Why will it work this time vs all the other times they've tried to overcome their problem and achieve their 'success island'?

When you're able to answer this question properly, you now hold that magic wand with the 'if' caveat.

Don't be afraid to own that magic wand. You must be confident in your ability to help solve the problems of your ideal client.

And of course, your ideal client won't be the 'trouble maker', your ideal client is someone who wants the solution but isn't afraid of doing what they need to do to get it.

14

Keeping the Magic Alive

Don't Push Away Your Prospects

In the early days before I'd mastered my sales I'd have this awful habit of trying to make sure my prospects had the money to pay me. My Sales and Leadership Coach, Jessica Lorimer, said this to me when I went through this stage of putting my 'dukes up' from the very outset with my audience, she said – 'don't hit them around the head with the sale before they've even got through the door.'

There is a right and a wrong time to prequalify your ideal clients and I was so hell bent on prequalifying the right people before they got on the sales call with me that I'd push people away before they'd gotten a chance to build trust. Meaning that even if they did have money, they were loathed to give it to someone who was mentioning it before we'd even got down discussing the possibility of the offer.

One of the biggest lessons she taught me was that it is none of my business how much money people have or even IF they have money. Don't prequalify on money, if you have something that is truly wanted, people will usually find the money from somewhere. It's whether they're willing to find it or spend it that's usually in question. You will automatically prequalify a lot of your clients through your messaging, and of course you will (or should) be taking people through a pre-qualifying questionnaire/application that mentions finances before you speak to them on the phone to weed out the tyre kickers, brain pickers and those that want the magic pill without the 'if'. If you're being transparent about your prices and you use the pre-qualifying questionnaire prior to the call, you'll 9 times of 10 end up speaking to the right people who will pay for your services.

Don't Convince

The other thing you need to avoid at all costs is the big convince. There is a difference between inspiring your prospects, showing them the transformation that's possible for them - and convincing them that they should be working with you.

There is a fine line and you don't want to be too far into the 'I'll let them make their own minds up' camp as that can lead to poor and lazy sales and marketing. But do check in and make sure that your marketing is speaking to the right person and is demonstrating what can be achieved for your ideal client without 'shouting' at people to buy your stuff. No one likes a desperate and needy coach.

When you have the magic solution for your prospects it will bring new hope to them and they will be more inclined to invest, because it's something they've not tried before, and their scepticism is minimised.

Creating Magic in Your Business

One great way to bring magic into your business is through creating unique systems, methodologies, infographics that explain unique big ideas that are simple to follow and easy to understand.

That last part - 'simple to follow and easy to understand',

is critical for it to appear 'magical.' Whether that idea is new to them or not, it will still appear 'new' because of how it's presented. Taking an idea, taking it apart and putting it back together in your unique way will 'tell it' in a way that may now make a whole world of sense. It allows people to take action and implement, bringing unbelievable value and provides the logic behind their emotional draw to buy from you.

15

How to be Wanted

Do I really have something that people want?

If you have an audience (i.e. an email list of prospects or a group) test it out. Ask them! Make sure that the audience you are asking are meant to want it. This might sound like a strange thing to say when you're testing the viability of something - but market research only works when you identify 'WHO' would need your offer in the first place and why.

If you were to throw the idea out to all your friends and family on Facebook, you'll get a million and one different responses, but are they the people that would really benefit from it in the first place? Probably not.

For those of you who don't have an audience the test will be on how quickly you're able to pull one together. If they like your lead magnet, which should be designed around helping someone solve a bleeding neck issue that is stopping them from achieving their overall success island, then you know that it's good sign that you have a wanted product.

Just for info - a lead magnet is something you create to give for free in exchange for some personal contact information such as their email address or access to contact via a chat bot, once you have their contact details you can then send them marketing and sales material.

Identify who would benefit from your offering and solution and test it on them. Sometimes you only get the truth of the matter when you start to actually sell the offer, which is why it's so important you don't physically create it before you've sold it. Design your product (packaged services) in principle as an outline. Reason being, if you spend months and months creating it to find that actually people were just being 'nice' saying they wanted it, when actually they're not willing to spend any money on it, you've just wasted a lot of time. People only truly value something when they're willing to part with their hard-earned cash.

Another sure way to know if you've hit the nail on the head with your offering is asking yourself 'would you pay for what you're promising?', this is very different to 'would you pay YOUR services?' Remove yourself as the person delivering the goods from the equation for one moment and just ask the first question again. Would you pay for the result you're offering? If you can answer this with absolute honesty and the answer is yes, then you can be sure that there will be others out there like you. And if you then find that it doesn't take well with others, you need to investigate whether you have the 'right' audience and have you positioned it correctly using the 'cocktail' approach.

The only way you'll know for sure if someone is willing to buy what you have to offer is to find a real person with a genuine problem and a true desire and package your services up as best you can using the knowledge in this book to solve that problem and achieve their desire and go sell it. If one person wants it, that is a sure-fire sign that you have a wanted product. It may just need some tweaks to make it more magical and desirable, and perhaps communicate the value and transformation better.

It's also likely that your ideal client was you at some point in your journey. You may have invested time, energy or money in help or experience to find the answers that you now supply. If that's the case you have a perfect marketing subject right there, YOU!

Ask yourself the following questions about your ideal client to gain further clarity on who this person is and what motivates them...

- Why is the outcome I provide, a priority for my ideal client?
- What will happen when my ideal client get's this outcome? What's the direct impact and the further impact achieving this will have? Think about the impact on finances, relationships, health, mindset, family etc.
- What will be your ideal client's fate should they decide to not get help? What's the 'hell' situation that will ensue. Again, direct impact and further impact on the rest of their life?

'Your value does not decrease based upon someone's inability to see your worth.'

Daniel Priestley, author of the incredible book Key Person of Influence wrote an incredible article based on this statement.

He claims that it isn't completely true, and I totally agree with him. Here's a snippet of what he says:-

"It's a nice idea but it's not actually true especially when it comes to business.

In the real world, if someone doesn't see your worth, they don't buy from you or hire you. If they don't see your worth they shop around, they negotiate on price they ask for free services.

In the real world, no one cares about how much value you place on yourself – they care about how much value they can recognise.

Fortunately, you are in control of what people can see. You have the power to pitch yourself more powerfully, you have the power to publish content that demonstrates value, to create and package products that solve meaningful problems, to show up more prominently online/offline and to build great partnerships with other influencers in business."

Source http://www.keypersonofinfluence.com/value-not-decrease-based-upon-someones-inability-see-worth/

Self-worth should not decrease and your ability to help someone does not decrease if someone can't see it, but your monetary value does. You will only ever earn what someone is willing to pay. Of course, if the person you are talking to isn't the appropriate prospect to need your product, it is not a reason to start lowering your prices. It's about offering your product to the *right* person who will pay good money for it because they need it and it's truly valuable to *them*, but if that ideal prospect can't 'see' the value then they're not going to pay for it.

And equally, if you're too cheap that person who could absolutely benefit from your services may not pay for it. There are certain types of high-end clients who won't touch you if you're too cheap. They'll be sceptical of your skill level and may not want to be associated with someone who charges below their worth. It's crushing but it's true.

"Sell them what they want, give them what they need."

For your ideal client to benefit from your services you need to angle it in a way that speaks to their desires. You may know that they need something, but they are blinded by what they think they need. As an example, my ideal clients need a micro-niche but what they want is to attract clients with ease by being the go-to expert in their field. I could choose to try and sell micro- niche and struggle for clients or I could choose to market to their want to become that client magnet, and during that process I'll help them niche down anyway because that's what is needed to become a go-to expert. If this book was called 'Micro-Niche to Success', it wouldn't have half the appeal because there is no emotional connection.

You are still going to give them what they want but you'll also give them what they need, so it's completely within integrity to do so.

What am I really solving?

Fred Smith, the founder and CEO of FedEx struggled to make money from his business in the first few years. He held strong to his idea of overnight delivery being a solid wanted service even though the take up was small and he was told repeatedly that it wouldn't take off. He knew that if it was needed by the few who had bought into the idea then there was hope and he was going to do everything he could to help it take shape. It was an unknown innovation at the time and people had to 'learn' that they could indeed benefit from it. Smith realised that the success of FedEx was laying in the hands of the positioning. Once he'd cottoned on that he wasn't selling transportation of goods (an external problem) and that he was indeed selling 'peace of mind' (an internal problem) and the marketing message was tweaked accordingly, the success of FedEx took off.

People are much more motivated to solve an internal problem, so whatever external problem you solve, have a think about the magic solution you bring to the REAL problem, the one that's keeping them up at night.

Once you've brought the magic of the new solution to them,

to achieve the thing they really want, to become the person they want to be, to solve the problem they'd give anything to solve, you'll have it positioned in such a way they'll find it a hard offer to turn down.

INGREDIENT 5: INTEGRITY

16

Authenticity - The Art of Integrity

Integrity is the final ingredient but it's by no means the least. Integrity by its very meaning has to be pulled through everything in your entire business from the brand, persona, life and business culture.

The definition of integrity according to the English dictionary is as follows: -

1. 'the quality of being honest and having strong moral principles.'
2. And 'the state of being whole and undivided.'

This definition is exactly what I'm talking about in this last section.

Integrity is having your thoughts, feelings and actions in total alignment. When you operate from this space, you operate from a place of total authenticity. The decisions you make are the right decisions that you don't have to second guess, the actions you take no matter how scary or impactful will be actions made from a good place, if of course, your thoughts are coming from a good place. Treat people as you'd treat yourself, but first make sure you're being reasonable with yourself. Are you being fair to you? Check in with yourself, know your boundaries, what do you want from the world and those around you, truly? *Then* treat people as you'd like to be treated.

Integrity, by its very nature, *requires* authenticity.

When you can harness integrity, it will be the unignorably unique scent that you leave where ever you go.

Integrity requires strength and courage to pull off, and this in turn requires you to be a true leader in your field.

Being in integrity requires you to have an opinion on the things that matter to you in your field and to stand for them. It means speaking up, it means walking the talk and it means being strong in what you believe even when others disagree.

You simply cannot be successful and pull yourself apart from everyone else out there by sitting on the fence, staying silent, softening the blow and changing with the wind to suit others who disagree.

It is imperative that you decide what you stand for, what you stand against and then follow through in the messages you put out there AND in the actions you take in your business.

There are so many out there who are preaching one thing and doing another. This will lead to mistrust from your followers and a bad reputation.

You must realise that not everyone will agree with your way of thinking and approaching life or business but there will be those that do. To resonate with those that do, we must put ourselves on the line and communicate what those stand points are.

17

How To Get Noticed

Polarising is essential if you want to stand out in the marketplace. Firmly standing up for something that you believe in that will either turn people ON or OFF, no in between.

This is the art of being Marmite! AKA Polarisation.

It's imperative we understand that to grab attention, get noticed and build a tribe of raving fans, we must have an opinion and we must NOT under any circumstances be BORING about it!

I want to give you some tips so that you can go about polarising positively.

- Do it with authenticity. People can smell attention seeking for the sake of it a mile away and you'll succeed in turning more people off than on. You want to be noticed for the right reasons not the wrong ones.
- The right people (aka the action takers that you can add value to AND monetize) will step up to a positive label. It has been proven in experiments that action taking people who are given a positive label will be more likely to step up to the plate and display the positive

behaviour and take the action that corresponds. So, for instance, saying that you will only work with people who are willing to do what it takes will help the right people step up and the wrong people float away or in some circumstances flounce off in an angry strop.

- Stand for something that you truly believe in! It doesn't matter if someone disagrees, all opinions are subjective, it's not about being right or wrong, it's about stating what YOU KNOW to be true in your experience. If you get haters, you know you've done your job.

If you're polarising authentically, within integrity for genuine stand points, then you can sleep soundly at night. And you can learn to celebrate the haters. You'll be being noticed for the right reasons and making more of an impact than if you have a bland message.

Here's an article that I wrote that caused a lot of controversy and not everyone agreed with, but I stand by every word.

"The BIGGEST LIE women business owners are told!

'If you don't sacrifice for what you want, what you want will be sacrificed.'

I totally agree with the statement above. So many women are sold the lie that 'you can have it all,' the problem is, 'all' is subjective from person to person.

A 'few' minutes of kindle time to my 5-year-old is lot more than the 'few' I was meaning.

When we hear the likes of Gary V shouting messages about 'hustle and grind,' the over-worked mother and business owner can get angry because the only thing they feel like they have left to give, is blood! And when we hear the likes of James Wedmore talk about a business by design that works for you, so you can release time to do the things you love, it makes you want kiss him. Both of these people polarise perfectly, and I love them both!

But in the wrong hands, both these pieces of 'advice'/messages will ruin your success. The lazy excuse maker will lap up James Wedmore's message and the workaholic could take Gary's message and run themselves into the ground taking pointless action and hitting burnout.

Here's what I believe as a mother of a 5-year-old and as a serious business owner.

You can't have it all!

You can't live your life at a perfect balance of zero, nothing would ever get done. A business is hard work and it WILL eat into your family/social time particularly in the beginning when you're testing out what works and what doesn't, and to be honest, that trial and error never really stops because it's essential to watch your business grow.

Having a business isn't for the faint hearted, in fact if you want to be able to have totally uninterrupted family time, you'd be better off getting a job where you can leave your work at the door and go and enjoy your holiday.

Now don't get me wrong, I'm not saying I don't spend quality time with my daughter and partner, I absolutely do, but unless there's a crisis or an emergency I put my business at the same level as I put them.

I know that last line will probably shock and put off a few people but at the end of the day if you want a successful business you have to be willing to put in the work where it's needed and put in the boundaries of where to stop so that you can ensure you spend that IMPORTANT time with your loved ones and with yourself, doing the things you love. But it'll never be perfect; some weeks you'll be working what seems like 'all hours,' others will be less, and you can spend more time nurturing personal time. But to think it will be a perfect and consistent schedule where you never break the 'it's 5pm so it's time to stop' rule on the odd occasion isn't realistic when it comes to creating success. I used to pay a significant amount on childcare so that I could spend the necessary time on my business. If you're starting a business because you want to spend more time with your kids... you're kidding yourself. Yes, it provides more flexibility, but those hours still need to be put in.

I see so many people using the excuse (yes, I said excuse) of family time because they've lost passion for their business, or they don't really know WHAT they should be doing to grow their business, or in fact have no interest what so ever in growing from where they are.

For those that want to grow and build an empire business and become a name in the market, you must be IN LOVE with the game, you must have a game plan and you must be committed to playing it, win or lose!

I'm the kind of person who needs boundaries to stop work, because continuous pointless action WILL lead to burnout and neglect, but I still very much believe in Gary's message. I do what is necessary to see the results that I want. It's all about priorities.

My message – Don't expect ALL the success if you work when you 'feel' like it."

So, did it push your buttons? Or do you agree?

Revisit your core message with this knowledge of polarisation and see if you can add some punch to your message.

18

The Art of Being You

A lot of people have difficulty with 'being themselves.' Many people hire copywriters to write their stuff, they edit their content and water it down so they don't annoy anyone. They copy the same approaches as everyone else so as not go against the grain and meet disapproval. They get stuck in perfectionism because 'god forbid their audience sees the real them'!

No one else can be you, you can't be put into a box. There is only ONE Jen Hall and there is only one YOU. You are utterly unique and what you bring to the table will be delivered in an entirely unique way.

When it comes to finding *your* uniqueness, Helen Packham, thought leadership expert, puts it perfectly. 'When everyone is going right, you go left.'

Take a long look at the common themes in your industry. The messages, the subjects, the style, the methods, the approaches, the opinions and find an authentic detour that will stand you apart from the crowd.

One of the best ways to go left, is to address a common

complaint from consumers in your industry. People try so hard to avoid complaints but in fact, if you can harness solving a common complaint, you'll be adding huge weight to your unique value proposition. You'll be solving a common problem that people experience and are trying so hard to avoid. It's a huge objection that you're overcoming from the outset, this breaks down the barriers immediately and gives you a unique edge over the other experts in your field.

Uncover Your Secret Weapon

I challenge you to get to know yourself so well that you uncover your secret weapon. There will be something about you, a skill, your personality, a quality that is so second nature, and second to none, that you will be able to leverage to pull yourself out of the dark and into the spotlight. You might have a hidden talent for creating epic videos, a knack for interviewing or being interviewed, inspirational speaking, writing awesome copy, being unbelievably entertaining, the list could go on. When you find your secret weapon and use it coordination with your marketing efforts, you can launch yourself into becoming 'known' in your field.

There is no room in this arena for those that aren't willing to step out. Introvert, or extrovert, quite frankly, whatever! People buy from people and unless you're willing to step out you'll never be noticed, and you'll never be seen as THE go-to expert.

Uncover your secret weapon - the one thing that if you master really well, you'll reach the mountain peak faster, leaving an avalanche in your wake.

Your Values

Your values determine what you stand for and how you polarise people. You have to be willing to take courage here. So many people are afraid to own their values through fear of being judged by others. The truth is, you will be. It's time to get over it and realise that not everyone is 'your kind of person' and conversely, you are not everyone's kind of person either. In the beginning it will hurt, because you are human, and you have feelings. But the more experienced and exposed to it you become the more self-aware and comfortable you feel in your skin.

If you're unwilling to stand for your values, you are disrespecting yourself and the rights that you have to be who you want to be in the world. Show yourself the same respect you would others; you're entitled to an opinion and the truth is, if you're not willing to express it, you are going to struggle in business.

People have to resonate with your values to connect with you emotionally – remember people buy emotionally first.

My incredible Sales Coach Jessica Lorimer holds 'integrity' and 'transparency' as two of her highest values. These values are exactly what made me want to work with her. Her belief in simple sales without sleaze drew me closer and had me hooked to find out more and very quickly allowed making the decision to work with her a very easy decision indeed.

Values are an integral part of standing apart from the crowd, but they are no good stuck on a piece of paper or inside your head, you must be able to action them.

My 2 biggest values in my business are Courage and Integrity. I action these inside my business all the time. Here are some examples of what I mean by actioning them...

- I take courage by doing the things that I know will have a positive ending but takes ovaries of steel to attempt and throws me completely outside my comfort zone. Such as contacting big influencers and building relationships with them. This was a huge deal for me, I was shaking in my boots the whole time, but I did it and it's done wonders for my confidence and career as a coach.

- On a weekly basis I make it a point of saying something that I believe strongly in that will potentially rock the boat with some people. I say what needs to be said even though it's scary!
- I act with integrity by always doing the right thing in my business even no one is looking. I treat all my clients with respect and treat them fairly. I deliver on my promises and I don't sell what I can't help someone achieve.

Action

- What values are important to you?
- What do you stand for?
- How will you uphold them in your business?

Here's another article I wrote around the time of the #metoo campaign. This came after watching an interview on the TV between a journalist and someone from the notorious Loaded magazine who is known for objectifying women.

"Loaded Mags Bold Move During the #MeToo Campaign

This morning as I was waiting to drive Andy and Ellie to their swimming session (aka let's go down the flumes as many times as humanly possible whilst Mummy writes an email) ...

I was flicking and stumbled across an interview with a writer from Loaded Magazine talking about the part they're playing in changing the way males view women following the #metoo campaign.

As some of you may be aware Loaded have notoriously in the past depicted women as 'objects' and 'eye candy' but today this awesome writer came out and made a bold promise about how they are going to operate moving forwards...

He declared that 'he believes that the modern man should be changing the way they see women as eye candy and objects at their disposal, and as such they are choosing to remove the glamorised photo shoots and 'eye candy' from their magazines, which has been one of the biggest reasons why some men have chosen to purchase that mag. He stated that they no longer want to serve the readers who want that kind of photography.

This was a bold move indeed, but one that I KNOW will pay off if continued to be executed correctly.

He, (they), were brave enough to state their new direction clearly and explained WHY! He stated what he believed... and because he stood up and stated what he believed, it sends a STRONG message out there that will attract a new more evolved reader and help their current readership step up to the new standards and get on board with this way of thinking. It's a mission to change the thinking of men and to provide a better standard of content in line with this thinking.

They want their readership to be proud of buying their magazine not something that they feel ashamed of and they were bold enough to come out and state this. At a time when a lot of men are actually being incredibly triggered by this #metoo campaign, this is indeed a bold move.

They could have thought... 'we are going to lose all our readers, because this content that we're currently releasing is the exact reason why people buy from us' But they've realised that times are changing, the world views are changing, and they have to adapt. They also have a new leadership from the inside who have recognised that they don't want to be associated with this damaging and horrific view of women. They have stated with pride who and what they stand against.

When it comes to our businesses we must move away from being scared to change direction, to state exactly who it is we want to work with, to state what it is we want to help with and stand in our truth.

Silence will kill your business.

Communicating what you believe (regardless of whether that means changing direction) is imperative to its success, because people need to, and want to know what 'views' / 'identity' they are buying into.

It's imperative to attracting the RIGHT clients and being KNOWN for the legacy in which you want to leave.

The fear of niching, the fear of polarisation, the fear of looking stupid, the fear of being rejected are ALL keeping you small and keeping your success at arms-length.

It's time to decide what you stand for, the mission you're undertaking, the legacy you want to leave and the means in which you choose to deliver it.

Not deciding and not communicating those decisions is keeping you right where you're at, the smaller version of yourself!

Decide and shout it from the roof tops! Take action!"

One of the biggest lessons to take from this example is that they have stated clearly who and what they stand against. This is just as important as standing FOR something. When you identify the 'enemy' that others can relate to, it encourages people to join forces against the evil. This has to be done with class, integrity and also to be used like salt. Just a pinch! Too much and you'll tip the balance and leave a bad taste, but just enough of this and it'll clearly define what you stand for and help to create a movement toward a brighter future for your following.

19

Know, Like, Trust

'Trust is like the air we breathe, when it's present, no- body really notices it, when it's absent, everyone notices it.'
-- Warren Buffet

Trust is a vital component to becoming a go-to expert. People need to trust you enough to come to you for guidance and if they don't trust what you're saying or doing is within integrity they'll stop following you and they will sure as hell not buy from you.

Desperate icky attempts to get noticed will be seen as hype and will put off the very people you're trying to convert into followers and clients.

The best way to come up with controversial content that stays with the realms of genuine authenticity is to immerse yourself in the opinions of others. This might seem simple, but if you're only hanging out with mice instead of lions you're going to find it hard to work out where you stand. Listen carefully to what is being said by the 'opinionated', and you'll soon find your own authentic stand point and voice in line with your core message. One of my clients Anwin Mbah, who is an expert in helping small business owners take control of their finances and grow their bank balance, doesn't believe in budgeting. She believes in a spending plan and that budgeting just keeps you in a scarcity mindset. This is a great take on all the other bland messaging that's going on in her industry. But the best part is, she genuinely stands for this message, it's not created for the hype, it's an organic, authentic stand point.

Don't pretend to be the Expert

This is a difficult message for me to deliver to you, because we all have to start somewhere. True experts usually suffer with some kind of imposter syndrome because the more we know the more we realise that we don't know it all. The thing is, we'll never know it ALL! But we must teach / help with the things we know truthfully, we can.

Once you've decided on your micro-niche it's your responsibility to learn and develop in that area on a weekly if not daily basis. Become obsessed with learning all there is to know on your chosen area.

What I'm saying is, there is always room for improvement. Make learning a habit and make adjusting your sails accordingly a habit too. Don't be afraid to admit you were wrong. It's through our mistakes that we can become the true expert.

Read, attend events, take courses and invest in your own coaching and mentors.

Deliver on what you say you will deliver. Be bold of course as I mentioned in the magic pill section, but don't overpromise, instead, over deliver.

Like I said, you'll never know it all, but in the continuous pursuit of excellence you'll be within total integrity to call yourself an expert.

Shaken Not Stirred

Sorry, it had to be done! I couldn't get the whole way

through this book without getting that in somewhere.

This last part is perfectly summed up by this cliché Bond quote.

No one successful got to where they are by being boring. It's time you shook up your industry by being loud and proud, in your own unique way. There are people who are naturally brash and that works for them, there are people who have a powerful but incredible down to earth presence. Whichever 'presence' you're looking to portray and which ever one comes naturally to you, what ever you do, don't be quiet. Be noisy and be powerful.

Do not assume luck has anything to do with people's success, it's all leverage and engineering. Leverage your unique excellence and authenticity to engineer your success. As Daniel Priestley says 'Resources show up after resourcefulness'.

It's no one's fault but your own for the lack of awareness of your presence in the market. Stand up, be counted, take courage, step out, share your awesomeness and be willing to fall, because you will.

Becoming an unrivalled expert takes work. There are a lot of moving parts and it may feel like an overwhelmingly big task. But nothing worth doing was ever easy and if you take a small step everyday in the shoes of the unrivalled expert you want to become, you'll make more ground than you ever believed you could.

Shake things up authentically and be more YOU!

And remember... the world ain't seen nothin' yet!

NEXT STEPS...

Congratulations on completing the book! Here's what you can do next...

I'd love to get your thoughts and meet you properly so come and join my free community on Facebook – Unrivalled Experts, where we can connect, get exclusive access to regular workshops and be the first to hear about Expert Unrivalled events! www.facebook.com/groups/unrivalledexperts

If you'd like to get in contact with me, you can reach me at jen@jen-hall.com and myself or one of my team will respond as soon as possible.

If you're interested in receiving one to one coaching from me or joining one of my programmes, book in a Clarity Strategy Session with me at www.jen-hall.com/contact

You can find me on all the usual social media channels by searching my name or visit my website at www.jen-hall.com for more details.

Review Offer

If you've been inspired by this book it would mean the world to me for you to leave a review on Amazon. For every review left on Amazon I will offer a FREE 15 Minute Laser Coaching Session. Just leave your review and contact me at jen@jen- hall.com requesting the session.

ABOUT THE AUTHOR

Photography by Lidia Drzewiecka

Jen Hall - Business Coach, Author and Multi-Award Winning Speaker

Jen is on a mission to see entrepreneurs own their unique value and charge their worth. She has been an entrepreneur since the age of 19 years old and has helped many entrepreneurs create successful businesses through finding true clarity on what makes them unique and utterly valuable in their clients' eyes.

She works with coaches and consultants taking them through her simple '5 step system' to nail their micro-niche and USP so they can stand out from the saturated marketplace and become the unrivalled in-demand expert who earns their worth.

"It is rare you come across people who are genuinely inspiring and who really do deliver on what they say they do in a way that is 120% committed to ensuring they offer the absolute best they can for the person they are working with. Jen Hall is that person.

Not only does she have an innate talent for seeing your potential and how the future of your business could develop, making you think about things in brilliant and different ways, she is also incredibly easy and enjoyable to work with.

If you need some business inspiration, motivation and clarity, about where you are going, how you can get there and what results you can deliver then I couldn't recommend working with Jen enough." Jo Darby Public Speaking Expert

Recommended Reading

- Key Person of Influence by Daniel Priestley
- Oversubscribed by Daniel Priestley
- Smart Leaders Sell by Jessica Lorimer
- Building a Story Brand by Donald Miller
- Start With Why by Simon Sinek
- Purple Cow by Seth Godin
- All Marketers Are Liars by Seth Godin
- Known by Mark W. Schaefer
- Take Your Shot by Robin Waite
- The Tipping Point by Malcolm Gladwell
- The One Thing by Gary Keller
- The 5 Second Rule by Mel Robbins
- Breaking the Habit of Being Yourself by Joe Dispenza
- The Big Leap by Gay Hendricks
- The Success Principles by Jack Canfield
- The Power of Now by Eckhart Tolle
- The Prosperous Coach by Steve Chandler & Rich Litvin

Notes

Notes

Notes

Notes